Judi Curtin

Lily
at
Lissadell

THE O'BRIEN PRESS
DUBLIN

First published 2019 by
The O'Brien Press Ltd,
12 Terenure Road East, Rathgar,
Dublin 6, D06 HD27 Ireland.

Tel: +353 1 4923333; Fax: +353 1 4922777
E-mail: books@obrien.ie.
Website: www.obrien.ie

The O'Brien Press is a member of Publishing Ireland
ISBN: 978-1-78849-128-0

1 3 5 7 8 6 4 2

19 21 23 22 20

Photo credits:

Lissadell House copyright Sean Kennedy; used with permission; Constance Marcievicz and
her children courtesy of the McMahon family; Maeve de Marcievicz, source unknown;
Maeve de Marcievicz letter courtesy of Lissadell Collection; used with permission.

Cover and internal illustrations by Rachel Corcoran.
Printed and bound by Norhaven Paperback A/S, Denmark.
The paper in this book is produced using pulp from managed forests.

Published in

DUBLIN
UNESCO
City of Literature

Chapter One

'**I** dare you, Lily!' said Rose.

Hanora didn't say anything, but she's not brave like Rose and me. I knew she didn't think my idea was a good one.

'Do it,' said Rose. 'Martin thinks he's so great ever since his daddy bought that cow. Look at him over there with a whole bottle of milk to himself and his bread with cheese *and* butter on it.'

I looked at the boy sitting on the only bench in the schoolyard, with his lunch all spread out around him. For a minute I imagined what life would be like if my family owned a cow. My little sister Winnie could

have cream for breakfast and her thin cheeks would fill out and maybe her cough would get better.

'It might be funny,' said Hanora. 'But Martin will go mad.'

'All the more reason to do it,' I said, laughing. 'And anyway, he's always bullying the little ones and playing tricks on them so it's time he learned his lesson. Are you two coming to watch?'

'Wouldn't miss it for the world,' said Rose.

I ran over to the fence where the ground was all mucky, and scooped a small bit of dirt into my left hand. Then, with my friends one step behind me, I walked towards the biggest, scariest boy in the whole school.

Martin's mouth was full of bread and cheese when we stopped in front of him. Rose and Hanora were giggling nervously and he didn't like that.

'What's so funny?' he asked, spraying us with soggy, cheesy crumbs.

Hanora was right, I realised – Martin would go

mad. I was a little bit scared, but I didn't want my friends to see me back down – they expect me to be brave and funny all the time.

'There's something on your face, Martin,' said Rose, nudging me. 'It looks like muck.'

Martin wiped his already clean face with the back of his hand.

'Up a bit,' said Rose.

'And a bit more to the side,' I added. My fear was slipping away and I was starting to enjoy myself.

Martin was still rubbing his face as I took a step closer. 'No, it's on the other side,' I said, pointing with my right hand. 'Will I wipe it off for you?'

Before he could answer, I reached out and ran my mucky left hand all the way down his cheek, leaving a dark brown stain.

'There,' I said. 'All clean again. You're welcome, Martin.'

I'm used to playing tricks, and the most important part is keeping my face perfectly serious, but Rose

and Hanora were laughing so much they looked as if they were going to die. Some of the other boys came over to see what was going on.

'What happened your face, Martin?' said one. 'It's all mucky.'

'I know you love your cow,' said another boy. 'But does she sleep in your house with you these days?'

Martin stood up, looking confused. 'But Lily wiped...'

He stopped talking and I could imagine wheels turning in his brain as he slowly realised what had happened.

For a second I felt sorry for him. I didn't really mean him any harm – I only wanted to make my friends laugh. I held out my hanky so he could clean his face, but he didn't seem to want it.

'I'm going to kill you, Lily,' he said.

'You'll have to catch me first,' I called, as I ran off towards the other side of the yard.

'Don't bother with her, Martin,' shouted one of the

boys after me. 'She's only a stupid girl.'

I wasn't 'only' a girl, and I *definitely* wasn't stupid, but when I looked back over my shoulder, I was glad to see that Martin wasn't chasing me.

Hanora and Rose were breathless by the time they caught up with me. 'Come on,' panted Hanora. 'Play-time must be nearly over, and we haven't done any skipping yet.'

Before it was our turn to skip, two small girls came over and pulled at my skirt.

'She pushed me, Lily!'

'Only 'cause she pulled my hair first.'

'But that's 'cause she called me stupid-face.'

'She called me a b…b….baby – and that's not nice – tell her, Lily.'

The two little girls were crying by now, and it was hard to understand what they were saying.

'Hush now,' I said, taking out my hanky and wiping their dirty little faces. 'Pushing and hair-pulling and name calling are bold – and

you're not bold girls, are you?'

The two heads shook.

'No one's stupid,' I said. 'And I don't see any babies around here. All I can see are two little girls who love to be tickled. Who wants to go first?'

The two little girls screamed as they held hands and ran away across the schoolyard.

Hanora and Rose laughed. 'You're so good with the little ones, Lily,' said Rose. 'You always know how to make them forget their fights.'

'She's right,' said Hanora. 'You're going to be a great teacher.'

'Thank you,' I said. I couldn't keep the smile off my face. All I wanted was to be a teacher – it was my favourite daydream, and sometimes I even let myself imagine that one day it would really come true.

* * *

In the classroom, Martin was staring at me and shak-

ing his fist, but I didn't care. Martin acts tough, but I knew he was afraid of the Master, and wouldn't dare to come near me.

First we had arithmetic, and I got nearly all of my sums right. As usual, Rose and Hanora were the best in the class, and the Master gave them each a gold star in their copy books. I wasn't jealous, though, because I'm always best at reading and writing – and Mam says no one likes you if you're best at everything.

For the last hour of school, the Master brought the boys outside to play ball, while Miss O'Brien took the girls for sewing. Rose hates sewing and asked if she could play ball instead. She was wasting her time because the Master said no, and all the boys laughed at her. Sewing time is my favourite though. We sit in a big circle and we're let talk to the people next to us, or sometimes Miss O'Brien reads us a story. Hanora and I can do small, neat stitches so we're allowed to sew on real material, cut from old rags. Rose and everyone else have to do their sewing on squares of

newspaper so their hands get all black.

Rose, Hanora and I were whispering together when Miss O'Brien came over and asked to see our sewing. 'That's beautiful – as usual, Lily and Hanora,' she said to us, when we held our work out.

When Miss O'Brien saw Rose's work it was a different story. She slapped her knuckles hard with a ruler, and took the scrap of paper from her. 'That's only fit for the bin, Rose,' she said, marching to the corner of the room. 'So I'll put it where it belongs.'

I put my arm around my friend. 'I don't care,' she whispered to me as she rubbed her sore hand. 'Sewing is stupid – and so is Miss O'Brien.'

When I'm a teacher, I'm never going to be like that. I will help the children who aren't very good at things, and I will never, ever slap anyone.

* * *

After school, Rose, Hanora and I stayed back to help

the Master tidy the classroom. It was my turn to fill up the inkwells so Rose and Hanora tidied and swept and the Master put all the books back on the shelf.

'Soon we'll be lighting the fire,' said the Master. 'And that will mean more work for us.'

I love wintertime when the classroom is all cosy with the fire lighting. Mam hates it though, as everyone has to bring in a sod of turf, and we scarcely have enough for ourselves.

'And have you all got your stories ready for Monday morning?' asked the Master.

'Mine's nearly finished,' said Hanora.

'Mine's ... well ... I know what it's going to be about,' said Rose, who usually left things until the last minute.

'I've had mine ready for ages,' I said.

I'd started writing as soon as the Master told us that we had to read our work out to the whole class. My story was about three girls who get lost in the woods and find a tunnel into a secret underground world –

where all their dreams come true. I knew the Master would love my story. I knew he'd smile at me, and tell me what a good writer I was, and write 'excellent' at the end of the page in his beautiful handwriting. I like Saturdays and Sundays, but I couldn't wait for Monday to come.

Chapter Two

'Lily, are you still awake?'

'Yes, Mam, but don't wake Denis and Jimmy, they have the legs nearly kicked off me with their fighting.'

She sat down on the edge of the bed, and I could see her thin face in the flickering light of the candle.

'Lily, I have something to tell you.'

'What is it?' I asked as I sat up, suddenly feeling important. I treasured these quiet times when everyone else was asleep, and it was just Mam and me.

'You won't be going to school on Monday,' she said.

'But I can't miss school! I want to get a ribbon for attendance this year – and I've written a story specially, and I'm going to read it out to the whole class, and ...'

'I'm sorry, pet.'

I felt tears coming to my eyes, but how could I

make a fuss about missing one single day? Mam had so much to do and she was always tired. Maybe she needed me to help with the washing, and the vegetable patch and taking care of my two little sisters. Anne could be very bold, and Winnie was sickly, and cried a lot.

'If you need me to help you on Monday, I don't mind staying home, Mam,' I said. 'Maybe the Master will let me read my story on Tuesday instead, if I tell him what happened. Maybe ...'

'Oh, Lily,' said Mam. 'You won't be going to school on Tuesday either.'

'But—'

'You won't be going to school any more.'

'But—'

'You'll be starting work. It's all arranged.'

I probably shouldn't have been surprised. I was the oldest girl in the whole school, and while I dreamed of staying on for another year or two, and one day becoming a teacher myself, at heart I knew that was

foolish thinking. Ever since Daddy died, I'd known that my school days would be cut short so I could help Mam to support the family.

Over the past year, I had watched as my friends left school to start work. In the springtime Rose would be moving to Sligo to work in her uncle's shop. As soon as her aunt sent money for the ticket, Hanora would be leaving for America, where all her big sisters and brothers were. Everything was changing much too fast for me.

'I know you'd like to stay on at school, pet,' said Mam. 'But that's impossible. This way I won't have to feed you, and your wages will be such a big help to us.'

I thought about my schoolbag, safely on the highest shelf, away from Anne's meddling fingers. I thought about my special story, and how much I wanted to read it out for the class. I could feel tears coming again, but how could I cry? How could I complain, when Mam had been raising five of us on her own

since Daddy died? How could I complain when she barely slept, and barely ate, and worked all day long, caring for us?

'Where am I going to work?' I asked quietly.

'It's a good position,' said Mam. 'In Lissadell.'

I'd never been to Lissadell, but I knew about it – everyone did. It was the biggest and fanciest house in our part of Sligo.

'But how did ...?'

'Your Uncle John knows one of the estate workers, and he arranged everything.'

Then I remembered something else. 'Lissadell is miles away. How will I walk all the way there, and do a day's work, and then walk home again before dark? Even if I walk my very fastest, that would be impossible.'

'Ah, pet,' said Mam. 'You won't be coming home at night. You'll be sleeping there – it's the only way.'

Now I did start to cry, remembering to be quiet about it so the little ones wouldn't wake.

'But I don't want to go,' I sobbed. 'I want to stay here with you, Mam. I can help you in the garden, so we'll be able to grow more food. I can—'

Mam leaned down and hugged me.

'It's how things have to be, Lily,' she said. 'You'll be leaving tomorrow afternoon, so you'll be ready to start work on Sunday.'

'But why didn't you tell me before now?'

'Maybe I should have, but I wanted you to enjoy your childhood for as long as you could.'

Was Mam saying that now I was an adult? If being an adult meant moving away and living far from everyone I knew, then I'd prefer to be a child forever.

'It's not too far away,' said Mam. 'And you'll have every Saturday off, so you'll be able to come and see us.'

'I will only see you on Saturdays?'

I'd never been away for even a day before, and the thought of six whole days without my family

terrified me.

'A whole day off is very generous – many houses allow their servants only a half day free. You're a lucky girl.'

I didn't feel lucky. I felt as if my life was over. Mam kissed me good-night, and then she took the candle and tiptoed from the room.

Chapter Three

'**I** think I'll do the washing today,' said Mam in the morning.

'But it's not Monday,' I said.

'No matter. It's a grand sunny day and the sheets will dry in no time.'

Mam loves when the two of us do jobs together. She loves the way we chat, and the way I make her laugh. Suddenly I understood how much she was going to miss me.

'I'll help you,' I said. 'Between the two of us we'll have the washing done in no time.'

And so we set to work, as my brothers and sisters played in the sunshine.

I usually hate doing the washing. The rubbing and wringing hurts my hands, and carrying the wet clothes makes my back ache. That day, though, I wished the

washing would never be finished. I wanted to stay there with my mam forever, scrubbing and rubbing all the long days.

Mam was extra-kind to me. When the washing was done, she spent ages brushing and plaiting my hair and she gave me extra colcannon at dinnertime.

* * *

Soon it was time for me to go.

'You could run over to see Rose and Hanora,' said Mam. 'You can tell them all about your new job.'

I shook my head. How could I say goodbye to my friends without crying like a little baby?

'No,' I said. 'Will you tell them where I'm gone – and that I'll see them next week?'

'I understand,' said Mam, and I felt tears coming to my eyes. Mam knew me so well. She could always guess when I had a headache, or felt sad about something. She knew when I needed a hug and a kiss,

even if I hadn't said a word. Mam had loved me all my life long, and now I had to go off into the world without her.

* * *

No one in our family had ever owned a suitcase so I had to use my schoolbag. I took the story I had written and hid it under the mattress. Maybe one day, things would be different, and I could go back to school. I put my reading book on the table in the kitchen and told the boys they could use it. 'But no scribbling or tearing pages, mind,' I said. 'It has to stay good enough for Winnie and Anne to have when they are older.'

Into the bag I put my change of clothes, my nightgown, my hairbrush and my prayer book.

Winnie and Anne cried when I told them I was leaving. They didn't understand how long a week was, and I think they would have cried more if they had

known the truth. Half an hour is a long time when you're little like them.

I knew the girls would miss me. Winnie always sat on my knee in the mornings before I went to school, because I was the only one who could persuade her to eat up all her porridge. Sometimes I could even get Anne to behave herself, with hardly any backchat at all.

The boys were too old for crying, but I knew they'd miss me too. I was the one who helped Denis with his sums, and Jimmy with his reading. I was the one who sorted out their silly fights. I was the one who washed their cut knees when Mam was too busy to help.

What would they all do without me?

Would Denis know that he had to be a help to Mam, now that he was the oldest child in the house?

Would any of them know how to make her laugh, when all the work and hardship was too much for her and it looked as if she was going to cry?

'Before you know it, it'll be Saturday again, Lily,' said Mam. 'And you'll be back to see us. We might not even recognise you. I suppose you'll be talking all fancy and will be full of airs and graces.'

I knew she was trying to make me feel better, but it wasn't working.

'Be a good girl,' she said. 'Do everything they tell you, and never forget your place. Don't let them see your skittish side – they won't like that.'

'What do you mean?'

'Oh, Lily, you know we love every single bit of you. We love how you joke with us and make us laugh – but in Lissadell, they won't want to see that. You're there to work, not to entertain them.'

I didn't like the sound of this at all. What if I got things wrong? What if they didn't like me?'

'So I have to become a new person?'

'Not new, just a little bit different. Watch what the other servants do. Remember to be nice, and then people will be nice to you. Now go along, or you'll be

late – you don't want to be walking on your own in the dark.'

I hugged her for a long time. When I pulled myself from her arms I saw that she was crying. I did my best to smile. 'Bye, Mam. Bye, children,' I whispered, and then I ran away, so I wouldn't cry too.

* * *

I felt strange as I walked along the lane in my Sunday dress, my mam's best shawl and my only boots, which didn't have any holes in them, but were made for a girl with smaller feet than mine.

I soon came to the schoolhouse, which was all locked up and empty. On Monday morning, Hanora and Rose and all the other children would arrive, and I would be far away, living another life. I wondered who would sit at my desk, and use my inkwell? Who would hang their coat on my hook? Whose story would the Master like the best? Who would be in

charge in games of Pickey, and make sure that everyone got a fair turn?

I'd never been anywhere on my own before, and I
wasn't sure I liked it. If the little ones were with me,
I could have listened to their chatter. If Hanora and
Rose were there I could have put on funny voices and
made them laugh. But I was on my own, and I had a
long walk ahead of me.

* * *

I'd been walking by the seashore for a long time. I
collected some pretty shells for Winnie and Anne,
and as I put them into my pocket, I almost managed
to forget where I was going, and why. Then I came
around a bend, and when I looked through the trees,
I broke one of Mam's rules and let my mouth hang
open. I couldn't help it – in front of me was the biggest and grandest house I had ever seen.

I started to walk away from the water towards the

house, but then I stopped. Once I entered that place, my childhood would be over forever – and I wasn't quite ready for that.

After looking all around, making sure no one else was on the beach, I took off my boots and my stockings and put them on the stone wall. Then I held up my skirt and ran towards the sea. The water was cool and fresh on my sore feet and I wanted to stay paddling forever. I found some flat stones and skimmed them on the surface of the water, the way Daddy had shown me when the whole family went on a big adventure to Rosses Point. Thinking about that special day made me sad, so I tried to concentrate on the sea and the soft wind and the seagulls squawking over my head.

When my arm was sore from skimming stones, I put on my shoes and stockings and followed the path leading towards the Big House. As I came closer, I felt as if I had no right to be in such a fancy place. I was afraid that someone would come along and chase

me away – but then maybe that wouldn't be the worst thing ever – I could go back to Mam and tell her the whole thing had been a big mistake.

But no one came, so I continued walking, half afraid to look at the windows, in case I'd see someone watching me.

I made it safely to a huge wooden door, which was much higher than the roof of my own house – it was big enough to drive a pony and trap through, which seemed very strange to me. While I stood there wondering if I should knock, a fine gentleman in a fancy suit came up behind me. He stood looking at me without saying a word.

'Excuse me, sir,' I said politely. 'Are you the owner of the house?'

He threw his head back and laughed which I thought was very rude. I could feel my face going red. I must have looked a sight in my too-small boots, with my dress damp from paddling, carrying my schoolbag and looking as if I was just about ready

to die. Maybe the man felt sorry for me because he stopped laughing.

'Unfortunately I am not the master of the house,' he said. 'My name is Albert and I am the baronet's driver.'

I didn't know what a baronet was, and I didn't want to appear foolish by asking, though maybe I looked more foolish standing there saying nothing. (At least I remembered to keep my mouth closed.)

'Dare I say you look a little bit lost?' he asked.

Now that he was being kind, I really wanted to cry, but I was afraid if I started I would never be able to stop.

'I'm the new housemaid,' I said. 'And I don't know where to go.'

'Well, you don't go in that door,' he said. 'That door is only for the gentry.'

'It's a huge big door,' I said. 'Are the gentry very tall?'

I could see by his face that was a stupid question,

but he didn't laugh at me. He pushed the door so it opened a little bit.

'Look inside,' he said.

I peeped through the door and saw a big space, with another huge wooden door opposite. On the right were six steps up to another smaller set of doors.

'I don't understand,' I said. 'Why are there so many doors? Why do some of them look as if they were made for giants?'

'This is called a *porte cochere*,' he said. 'When a carriage or a motor car comes, it drives right through the first big door, so when the people get out they're not blown away with the wind and the rain. The passengers go up those steps into the house, and the vehicle drives out the other side.'

'It's so fancy,' I said. 'I've never seen anything like it in all my life. But if I can't go through there, how do I get inside the house?'

'You go in by the servants' tunnel.'

'A tunnel especially for servants!'

'It's not so special. It's so the gentry won't have to look at the likes of us coming and going.'

That sounded very strange to me. Why wouldn't the gentry want to see me and Albert? I was in my Sunday best and his suit was very smart. I didn't want him to think me stupid, though, so I didn't ask any more questions.

I looked around, but I couldn't see any sign of a tunnel. Albert was a kind man, so he walked around the house with me, and showed me the entrance to a long, dark passageway.

'Off you go,' he said. 'You'll end up in the court-yard. Just knock on the first door on your left, and one of the servants will let you in.'

Chapter Four

J knocked quietly, and when nothing happened, I knocked again, this time a little louder. After a minute, the door opened and in front of me stood a red-headed girl of about my age. She was wearing a white apron over a stiff black dress and a funny white cap. She had a face on her that would turn milk sour.

'Well?' she said, folding her arms and staring at me. 'What do you want?'

'I'm the new housemaid.'

'That would be *under* housemaid,' she said. 'You'd better follow me.'

I wasn't very happy about following this grumpy creature, but I didn't feel like arguing with her either, so I trailed along a corridor after her until she stopped outside a black door.

'Wait here for Mrs Bailey, the housekeeper,' she

said, and then she knocked once on the door and flounced off the way we had come.

By now my feet were killing me, and the sand from the beach was irritating my blisters. There was a chair next to me, but I didn't dare to sit down. I didn't dare to do anything but stand up straight, and try not to look as if I were about to faint away from hunger, tiredness and fear.

'Come.'

It was a woman's voice from inside the door. Was she talking to me? Or was she calling to her pet dog? I hopped up and down on my sore feet, trying to decide what to do, when the voice came again, louder and a bit impatient-sounding, 'Come!'

I opened the door and took a single step inside. It was a big bright room, and I could see a woman sitting behind a desk. She smiled at me, and once again I could feel the tears coming. Why did nice people make me cry? I realised I had no one to ask about this, and that made me want to cry even more.

'You must be Lily.'

I nodded, too afraid to speak.

'I'm Mrs Bailey,' she said. 'You are welcome to Lissadell. If you work hard here, you will get along very well – and you won't have to be an under housemaid forever, you know.'

'Yes, Mrs Bailey.' I wasn't looking forward to being an under housemaid so it was good to know it wasn't a life sentence. I wondered what else I could be, but didn't dare to ask. What would she say if I told her that I really wanted to be a teacher?

Mrs Bailey took a big book from a shelf, and turned to a new page. Then she wrote down my name and my address and my date of birth. She asked me if I could read and write, and I told her I could. Then she asked me what sewing I could do, and I proudly told her all the things Miss O'Brien had taught me. When I told her I was allowed to sew on material instead of newspaper, she laughed, and I felt a bit stupid. I suppose rich people like her never have to

sew on newspaper.

When she was finished writing, Mrs Bailey rang a bell, and a minute later the door opened and another maid came in. This girl was dark-haired and pretty and she had a lovely friendly smile.

'Isabelle, please take Lily to her room and help her get settled.'

'Yes, Mrs Bailey,' she said in a quiet voice. 'Come along, Lily.'

I followed her along a corridor, past rooms packed with bottles and jars and all kinds of food. One room had shelves and shelves all full of fine china. There was a smell of freshly baked bread that made me feel weak. What I wouldn't give for a warm crust with a scrape of creamy butter!

At the very end of the corridor, Isabelle opened a door.

'Here you are,' she said, stepping inside. 'Home sweet home.'

It was a lovely room, with a window at one end,

and a small, metal-framed bed against each of the side walls. In a corner there was a narrow press, and near the door was a real fireplace.

'You'll be sharing of course,' said Isabelle. 'Every-one shares except for the housekeeper and the butler.'

'How many to each bed?' I asked, thinking if it were more than three it might be a bit of a squash.

Isabelle laughed. 'Oh, you are funny,' she said. 'You share the room, but the bed is your own.'

'I was only joking,' I lied. I remembered Mam's warning, and felt bad. Isabelle thought I was being skittish, even when I was being perfectly serious. I hoped I wasn't going to get a bad name, just because everything was so new to me.

Then I noticed that there was a small locker next to each bed.

'And I have a locker all to myself too! Do you think I could save up for a candle, and then I could read at night time?'

'No need,' said Isabelle pointing to the wall over

the fireplace. 'Lissadell is very modern. There's a gas light in every single room.'

I'd never heard of such a thing, but didn't want to say it.

'This is your bed,' said Isabelle, pointing to the left. 'And your uniform is all ready in the press.'

Suddenly I felt very lost and lonely. I sat on my bed and Isabelle sat down beside me and put her arm around my shoulders. 'I know everything is strange at first,' she said. 'But you'll soon get used to it.'

She was being kind, but it wasn't helping very much. I missed Mam and Rose and Hanora. I missed my home and my brothers and sisters. Everything was too different and too new.

'I don't know what to do,' I said. 'I've never been in a fine house like this before. It's so big, I'm afraid I'll get lost and never be seen again.'

Isabelle laughed. 'Trust me — everyone feels like that in the beginning. After a few days you'll be grand.'

'And I don't know what to say to all these fancy people.'

'Don't worry about that. You don't say anything to them unless they speak to you first – and usually they only say "good morning"or "good evening" and you say the same and then you go on your way. They don't want to be your friend or anything like that.'

'You make it sound easy – but I'm still scared.'

'You don't have to be scared. We're lucky to be working here – the Gore-Booths treat their servants well – not like some I've heard of. They are good people – and always have been.'

'What do you mean?'

'My daddy told me that way back in the famine times, some landlords did terrible things, but the Gore-Booths were kind, and helped to feed the starving people.'

I was glad to hear that my employers were kind, but I was still worried.

'And the work,' I said. 'I don't know what I'm sup-

posed to do, and I'm afraid of getting things wrong.
Will you be able to show me?'

'I'm sorry – I'm not a housemaid. I'm a children's
maid – I help the nurse to look after the little ones.
There's four of them, you know. They're very sweet,
but they keep me on my feet, I can tell you. I'm only
down here with you because they are all napping at
the moment.'

'So who will show me what to do?'

'Oh ... Nellie will help you for the first day or two,'
said Isabelle, not sounding very sure.

It took me a minute to understand, and then I
remembered the grumpy girl who'd opened the door
for me.

'Has Nellie got red hair?' I asked.

'So you met her?'

I nodded. 'She wasn't friendly like you. She was ...'

'You'll get used to Nellie. She's always in a bad
mood on Saturdays.'

That made me feel better, until Isabelle continued.

'And every other day too.'

Then I had a horrible thought. I pointed at the bed next to mine. 'Do you sleep there?'

'No. I sleep in the night nursery – in case the little ones need me. That bed is ...'

'Nellie's?' I asked.

'Yes. You have to understand, Nellie is ...'

'What?'

'Nothing. Now you need to get into your uniform. I'll go and call Nellie and she can bring you back to Mrs Bailey when you're ready. Look sharp – we've already spent too much time chattering.'

She went outside and closed the door. I took off my boots and put on the black shoes that were waiting for me at the foot of my bed. They weren't new, but someone had polished them until they shone – and they didn't hurt my blisters too much. I took off my own dress and got the uniform from the press. I'd never had a uniform before and for a moment I felt big and important as I slipped the stiff black dress

over my head. I didn't feel so good when I realised that the apron was a complicated piece of clothing, and I had no idea how to put it on properly. I was still trying to work it out when the door opened with a clatter and Nellie came in.

'Did you touch my things?' she said, staring at the locker next to her bed. 'You're never to touch my things!'

She was just a girl like me, but I couldn't help feeling afraid of her. She sounded so angry. She sounded as if she hated me, even though she didn't know me at all.

'No,' I said in a shaky voice. 'I didn't touch anything, I swear.'

'Well get a move on. Mrs Bailey is waiting.'

I still hadn't put on my apron or frilly white cap, and without a mirror, I didn't know where to start. Nellie grabbed the apron from my hands, put it over my head and tied the bows in the front, pulling them so tight they hurt. Then she took the cap from the

bed and rammed it onto my head.

'There,' she said with a smirk. 'That's perfect.'

I didn't like the way she said that. Maybe my hair was all sticking out or something, but before I could ask, Nellie was half way down the corridor, and I ran to follow her, afraid of getting lost on my own.

* * *

Nellie and I were standing outside Mrs Bailey's office, with our hands behind our backs. Mrs Bailey looked as if she was about ready to explode.

'Is this meant to be some sort of joke? Because if it is, I have to tell you I am not amused.'

I hadn't even said a word, so I knew she couldn't be blaming me – or could she? She was looking at me as if she wanted to give me a good shake.

'What is it, Mrs Bailey?' asked Nellie. 'Is something wrong?'

Mrs Bailey looked at Nellie, narrowed her eyes,

and then she spoke to me in a softer voice.

'Who told you to do your apron and cap like that?' she said.

Behind me, I could feel Nellie's fingers pinching my arm. She'd been mean and I wanted to get her into trouble, but I guessed that wouldn't end well for me. So I did something that always worked in the Master's classroom – I completely avoided Mrs Bailey's question.

'I've never worn an apron like this before,' I said. 'Or a cap either. And I didn't know the right way to put them on.'

Mrs Bailey took a long look at Nellie, and then she smiled at me. 'Well, I'm afraid this isn't the right way. I will show you once, and you will have to do it on your own from now on.'

She took off my apron, put it back on the other way around and tied the strings behind me. Then she took the cap off my head, turned it right way out, and put it gently back in place.

'Do you think you'll be able to manage that on your own?' she said.

'Yes, Mrs Bailey,' I said. 'Thank you.'

'Now, Nellie,' said Mrs Bailey. 'Lily is to follow you for the rest of the evening, and watch what you do, and she can start work proper in the morning. And mind you behave yourself. Off you go, the bedroom fires won't light themselves.'

I wanted to say that I was hungry, that I hadn't had any tea before I left home, but I was too shy and too afraid, so I rubbed my tummy to stop it from grumbling and I set off after Nellie.

* * *

Nellie stopped at the bottom of a curved staircase.

'After you,' she said.

I looked at the stairs twisting up and up, higher and higher. They were so steep, and so scary! The grey stone steps were worn black and shiny in the

middle. I wondered how many servants had gone up and down. I wondered how many of them had been afraid, like me.

'Keep moving, Lily, you've seen a staircase before, I hope.'

'Of course I have,' I said. This was true – once Mam took me to Sligo and I saw stairs in a hotel. Only thing was, I never had a chance to walk up those stairs. My house and my friends' houses and my school were all on one level, and the church only had three steps outside the front door. When it came to climbing stairs, I was still at baby infant level. I took a deep breath and held tightly to the handrail as I carefully followed the steps upwards. At the top, I felt as proud as if I'd climbed all the way up Benbulben, but I didn't tell Nellie that. I didn't want to give her a reason to laugh at me.

* * *

I followed Nellie around for what felt like hours. I watched as she lit fires and straightened eiderdowns and picked up clothes. There were so many rooms – and some of them were bigger than my whole house. Everywhere I turned there were rugs and soft couches and silk curtains with tassels on them. It was like being in a palace in a fairytale.

I thought of all the fun Rose and Hanora and I could have in this place – playing games and pretending to be fine ladies – but Rose and Hanora were far away. All I had was Nellie, who looked like she didn't even know what fun was.

One bedroom had a huge four-poster bed, piled high with pillows and eiderdowns and velvet blankets. Even looking at it made me feel tired. I wanted to kick off my shoes and jump in and wrap myself up in the softness, and sleep for hours.

Nellie grabbed my arm and pulled me out of the room. 'Stop dilly-dallying,' she said. 'We've got work to do.'

A few times I asked questions, but I soon learned that I was wasting my breath. Nellie either ignored me completely or looked at me as if I had grown two heads. Mam's advice about being nice to people wasn't working so far. I was being as nice as I could to Nellie, but the nicer I was, the more she seemed to hate me. In the end I just followed her around like a silent shadow. A few times I stuck my tongue out at her behind her back, but that didn't make me feel much better.

* * *

It was nearly midnight when I got to my bed. Within seconds Nellie was slumbering soundly, but even though I was exhausted, I had trouble sleeping. I'd never slept in a bed on my own before, and though I'd often dreamed of this, now that it had happened, I wasn't sure I liked it. I was used to the warmth of my brothers and sisters. I was used to Winnie's little

fingers twisting the hair at the back of my neck. I was used to the steady breathing of the four little people I loved most in the world. I was used to knowing that Mam was only feet away, ready to jump from her bed in the kitchen at the first sign that one of us needed her. And listening to Nellie's loud snores didn't make up for any of these things!

I wrapped myself up in Mam's shawl and tried to imagine that she was there, hugging me and making me feel safe. I lay and looked at the ceiling and tried to cry silently as I wondered if I would ever get used to this strange new life.

Chapter Five

'*W*ake up, Lily, wake up.'

Someone was shaking me roughly. 'I'm sorry, Mam,' I said without turning over. I was all confused. Did I sleep too late? Had Winnie eaten her porridge? Were the boys up? Was it time for school?

Nellie's harsh laugh reminded me that I wasn't in my own bed, my mam and my brothers and sisters were far away and there was to be no school for me ever again.

I jumped out of bed, afraid of getting into trouble for being lazy. The floorboards were cold on my bare feet, so I hopped up and down as I brushed my hair and put on my uniform. Nellie looked disappointed when I managed to fix my apron and hat correctly. I followed her along the corridor, hoping it was break-fast time. I was wrong!

She led me to a storeroom near the kitchen.
'There's your housemaid's box,' she said, pointing at a
big wooden box with a metal handle. 'Make sure it is
always correctly stocked.'

'Stocked with what?' I asked, sure it wasn't going to
be filled with books or sweets or anything nice at all.

Nellie rolled her eyes. 'With everything you need
for cleaning the grates.'

I picked up the box. It was heavy and awkward to
carry – and it wasn't any easier when Nellie shoved a
sweeping brush and a mop towards me. When I had
everything balanced, she picked up another box like
mine, took a mop and a brush and headed for the
back stairs.

'I'll do the dining room first, and you can do the
drawing room,' she said when we got to the top of
the stairs. 'And get a move on – this has to be done
before the family comes down for breakfast.'

She wasn't happy when I followed her into the
dining room.

'This isn't the drawing room,' she said. 'Have you a brain at all, or is your head filled with cotton wool?'

'I have more than enough brains, thanks for asking,' I said, as I put down the heavy box. 'But I'm not a mind reader, so if you won't tell me what to do, I'll have to watch you, and then go and do the same in the drawing room.'

Nellie seemed surprised, but she couldn't really argue with what I said, so she called out a big long list: 'Open the shutters. Shake the curtains. Clean and blacklead the grate. Light the fire. Dust everything. Throw damp tea leaves on the rugs. Sweep the rugs. Sweep the floor. Polish the floor.'

I knew how to clean – I'd been helping Mam for most of my life – but half the things Nellie said made no sense. What was blackleading the grate?

Why would you throw tea leaves on the rugs? It was messy and a terrible waste. (In our house, tea was a special treat for Sundays, and Mam used the leaves over and over again until the tea they made was like

pure water, and after that the leaves were put on the vegetable patch – we would never, ever throw them on the floor.)

In the end, I found a system that worked. I did the first thing on Nellie's list as fast as I could, then I ran next door to see what she was doing, and I copied that, over and over until at last the drawing room was clean and shiny, with a lovely fire burning in the grate. *I* wasn't very clean and shiny though – I looked like a wild woman from all the running around, and I had a big black stain on my apron.

Nellie came and looked at my work. 'That's not too bad, I suppose,' she said, which I think might have been a big compliment coming from her.

Just then Mrs Bailey came along.

'How is the work going, Lily?' she asked. 'Is Nellie showing you the ropes?'

I put my head down. What would Mrs Bailey say if she knew how I'd struggled with cleaning the drawing room – that mostly I'd had to work things

out for myself?

Nellie didn't say anything either, so Mrs Bailey must have guessed there was a problem.

'Let me spell it out for you, Nellie,' she said in a cold voice. 'Lily is new, and I want you to take her in hand today. There is a right way to do everything, and it is your job to show Lily what the right way is. For the rest of the day, you work on every room together. Is that clear?'

'Yes, Mrs Bailey,' said Nellie, giving me a vicious stare. It wasn't fair. I hadn't done anything wrong, and still Nellie seemed to have found one more reason to hate me.

I was very tired by now, but there wasn't any time to rest. Nellie had picked up her box and mop and brush and seemed to expect me to follow her.

'Just the bow room, the billiard room, the hall, the gallery and Sir Josslyn's study to do, and then we're finished ...' said Nellie. I felt a little bit better until she finished her sentence. '... downstairs.'

*   *   *

All the rooms were full of ornaments, and everything had to be picked up and dusted and put back in exactly the same place. Some of the shelves had glass cases full of dead butterflies and beetles. Nellie thought they were pretty, but I felt sorry for the poor creatures, all stiff and cold and pinned to cardboard forever.

After a while I walked into one room and saw a big brown bear standing up on his back legs, showing his huge sharp teeth and claws. I grabbed Nellie's arm, and screamed. 'A bear! Nellie, it's a bear! Run!'

'He scared me too at first,' said Nellie, laughing. 'But don't worry, Lily. He's stuffed. He can't hurt you. Look, you can touch him.'

I copied her and touched the fur on the bear's back. It was dry, and coarse – not soft at all.

'Is he real?' I asked. I realised I was whispering, almost as if I might wake him up.

'Of course he's real. He's been here for years and years. Some people say Sir Josslyn's father, Sir Henry, shot him. Other people say that the butler, Mister Kilgallon, shot him because he was attacking Sir Henry.'

I looked nervously out the window. 'I didn't know bears lived around here. If Mrs Bailey sends me to the kitchen garden to pick flowers, I'll have to bring Mr Kilgallon along to protect me.'

'You're funny,' said Nellie. 'Bears don't live here. Sir Henry went on long expeditions to the Arctic, and that's where this one came from.'

'Where's the Arctic? The Master at my school taught us a lot of geography, but it was mostly about the rivers and mountains of Ireland. Did you learn about the Arctic at school, Nellie?'

'No!' it sounded as if she didn't like my question, so I decided not to ask any more.

'Oh well, who cares anyway?' I said. 'All I know is, if the Arctic's full of angry bears with sharp teeth

like this one, then I'm *never* going there. I think I'll stay in Ireland and take my chances with foxes and badgers and field mice.'

Nellie laughed for a long time, and I realised that I hadn't heard her laugh before – it was a nice sound. But then it was as if she remembered who she was, and her laughing stopped. 'You're distracting me from my work,' she said. 'Stop chattering and start working – that's what we're here for.'

I looked at her for a second, confused by how she could be nice and happy one minute, and grumpy the next. There were so many things I wanted to say to her, but I didn't dare to say any of them. So I picked up my box and began to clean yet another fireplace.

* * *

By the time the downstairs rooms were finally done I felt as if I hadn't had a bite to eat for years, and I very much hoped it was time for breakfast. I was

wrong again.

'Now we do the dressing rooms,' said Nellie. It didn't seem fair. Mam is the hardest-working person I've ever known, but even she never does any work before breakfast. I felt sad as I imagined my poor tired mother sitting at the kitchen table with a bowl of porridge. I imagined her sighing as she scraped the bowl clean, saying – 'a good breakfast sets you up for the day, never forget that, Lily.' I could feel tears coming to my eyes, but I quickly wiped them away – I didn't want Nellie thinking I was a baby.

We had to go downstairs to empty the ashes out of our boxes. I followed Nellie through the kitchen, and tried not to look too longingly at piles of food laid out on big silver platters. Surely no one would mind if I helped myself to a small scrap of bread? After all, a housemaid who died of starvation wouldn't be able to do much work, would she? I didn't dare to take the chance, though.

'Who lives here in Lissadell?' I asked as we went

up two flights of stairs to where the bedrooms and dressing rooms were.

'The Gore-Booths, of course.'

'I *know* it's the Gore-Booths, everyone knows that – but who exactly are they?'

I half expected her to laugh at my question, but right then I learned something important about Nellie. She had a grudge against almost everyone in the world, but for some reason she was half in love with our employers.

'The master is Sir Josslyn,' she said. 'He's a baronet.'

'What's that?' I asked, remembering the word the driver had used the day before.

'That's ... that's ...' I wanted to laugh as I realised Nellie didn't know the answer, but then I felt sorry for her. In some strange way, I knew she was trying to impress me, so I decided to help her.

'I suppose baronet is some kind of title,' I said.

She nodded. 'Yes,' she said. 'That's it. It's definitely a title. It means Sir Josslyn is a very important man

– and he's a good man too – always very decent and polite. His wife is Lady Mary, and there never was a kinder woman walked this green earth. If it weren't for those two fine people ...'

She didn't finish, and that made me really want to know what she had planned to say.

'What?' I prompted, but she ignored me.

'The Gore-Booths are the best employers in all Ireland, and we are lucky to be here,' she said. 'Their children are Michael and Hugh and Bridget and little baby Brian. Perfect angels, they are, every last one of them.'

I smiled to myself. I didn't know if what Nellie said about the family was true, but as long as she loved them, I was prepared to love them. I was sad and lonely and ready to do almost anything to make this strange and grumpy girl like me.

'This is a very big house for two adults and their babies,' I said, thinking of Mam's tiny cottage, and how we all had to squash to fit in.

'Many visitors come to us at Lissadell,' said Nellie, as if people came to see her rather than Sir and his family.

'Who visits?' I asked. This chatty Nellie was much nicer than the grumpy one, so I wanted her to keep on talking.

'There are many friends,' she said. 'Important people from all over the country – poets and artists and the like. And Sir Josslyn's brother and sisters come from England with their children.'

'That's nice,' I said, still trying to keep the conversation going. 'Anyone else?'

'Well, there's Lady Georgina and Miss Maeve, but they hardly count as visitors, since they are here so often.'

'Who are they?'

Nellie gave me a scornful look, as if my question was a really stupid one. 'Lady Georgina is Sir Josslyn's mother. She used to live here, but she moved out so Sir Josslyn could get married.'

'She had to leave her own house so her son and his wife could have it? That doesn't sound very fair.'

'Sir Josslyn is very fair. He even allows Miss Maeve and Lady Georgina to keep their old rooms for when they visit – they just don't live here any more.'

'That still doesn't sound right to me.'

Nellie rolled her eyes. 'The oldest son gets the house. It's the way the gentry do things – you wouldn't understand.'

She was right about that. I thought about Mam. If Denis got married, he'd never, ever put her out of her own home. Maybe rich people didn't always have the best ideas. I knew Nellie wouldn't agree with me, and I didn't feel like a fight, so I changed the subject.

'Who is Miss Maeve?'

'Miss Maeve is Sir Josslyn's niece – she's the daughter of his sister, Countess Markievicz.'

At last a familiar name! Once, when Mam thought I wasn't listening, I heard our neighbor, Molly Carty, whispering about the countess. She had that voice

adults use when they are talking about shameful things, and I could hear interesting words like 'disgrace' and 'scandal.' I was dying to know more, but when Mam saw me edging closer she made a face at Molly and started talking about how cold the weather had been lately.

'Have you ever met the countess, Nellie?' I asked.

'Many times,' said Nellie, as if they were the best of friends.

'What's she like?'

Now Nellie looked all prim. 'We don't talk about her very much. *I* think she's a disgrace to the family.'

Now I was *very* interested, but we were already at the top of the stairs and Nellie seemed to think the conversation was over.

'You're not paid to gossip about the family,' said Nellie, as if she hadn't said a word. 'And you shouldn't be criticizing your betters.'

I hadn't criticized anyone, but her comment made me think. The Gore-Booths were definitely richer

than me, but were they really better?

'We've got work to do,' said Nellie. 'There are no visitors, so just two dressing rooms to do today.'

The dressing rooms were big and very fancy. I couldn't understand why anyone would need a special room, just for keeping their clothes and for getting washed and dressed in.

Talk of the family must have made Nellie feel generous, so she obeyed Mrs Bailey's order and showed me what to do. We scrubbed the washing basins, and laid out the soap and towels the way the Lord and Lady liked. Then we cleaned the grates and lit the dressing-room fires and tidied everything. After that, when I felt as if I had been working for weeks, Nellie said the sweetest words I had ever heard in my whole life.

'And now it's time for breakfast.'

Chapter Six

We had porridge for breakfast, just the same as at home, but I was so hungry it tasted like the finest sweets I'd ever eaten. Nellie and I were the only people in the kitchen, which meant I didn't have to talk, and I could concentrate on eating. I used my finger to pick up the last few grains of porridge, but stopped when I saw Nellie glaring at me.

A maid came to take away my bowl and I wondered why Nellie wasn't standing up to go. A second later the same girl came back in carrying two plates.

'Leftover meat pie from last night,' she said, as she put the plates in front of us. 'Cook goes mad when food is sent back from the dining room – takes it as an insult.'

I smiled. I didn't care if the cook felt insulted – the meat pie was delicious! I still wished that I was at

home, but I was beginning to see that life at Lissadell might have its compensations.

* * *

After breakfast, there was plenty more work to do, and once again I followed Nellie up the back stairs.

'This is where Lady Mary sleeps,' said Nellie. 'She's downstairs having breakfast now, so we can clean in here.'

We were in a bedroom that was about three times the size of my house. It was the most beautiful room I had ever seen, with three windows, and a big four-poster bed. If I had that bed, I'd pretend to be sick every single day of my life, so I could stay lying there on the beautiful silk pillows and sheets, looking out at the gardens and the mountains.

Making the bed took ages. All the blankets had to be shaken out, and the top mattress turned, and then the bed had to be made up again. Then we cleaned

the fire, dusted and polished everything and moved on to the next room.

After a while, I was so tired, I didn't care that Nellie had stopped talking to me. My arms and my back ached, and the blisters on my feet were hurting me. I felt as if it had to be bedtime, but as we'd just had breakfast, I knew that wasn't very likely. The day seemed to be going on forever.

* * *

Much later, when I was nearly ready to curl up in a corner and fall asleep, Nellie said it was time for dinner. We went into the servants' dining hall, and suddenly I felt shy. The room was full of servants, all lined up along a huge table, with men on one side and women on the other. There was no sign of Isabelle, and I wondered if I'd ever see her again. Maybe she had to eat with the children in the nursery. I wished I could be with her, instead of here amongst

all these strangers. Nellie went and stood behind a chair, and I hesitated, not knowing what to do. All I knew was that I didn't want to sit next to her, so I found a space on the women's side, near the middle of the table, and stood there. Suddenly the room went silent, except for one young boy who pointed at me and laughed out loud. I felt all hot and bothered, and could tell that my face had gone bright red. I knew I had done something wrong, but didn't know exactly what that was. Then a nice man who was standing opposite smiled at me and jerked his head towards the end of the table, where Nellie was standing.

'Housemaids sit down there,' he whispered.

'Thank you,' I whispered back, and feeling like a dunce, I moved toward the other end of the table. I noticed that as I walked, the servants were getting younger, and their uniforms were getting less fancy. It was a bit like school, where the silly little children all had to sit together at the front of the class, while the older, more important ones sat at the back. It was

strange, being one of the youngest again.

The line of chairs seemed to go on forever, as I walked slowly, still not sure which of the empty seats was meant for me. I saw a space on Nellie's right, and just as I got there, she turned and gave the tiniest nod. I smiled to thank her, and stood in the space, feeling happy that maybe, somewhere deep inside Nellie, there really was a heart.

There were two more girls standing on my right, and I wondered who could be even less important than me.

Just then, Mrs Bailey came in and stood at one end of the table, and a tall, very stern-looking man with white hair and a beard stood at the other. Mrs Bailey said grace and then everyone pulled out their chairs and sat down.

'Who's that tall man with the beard?' I asked the girl next to me.

'That's Butler Kilgallon,' she said. 'He's been at Lissadell for many, many years. He started work here

when he was ten years old!'

My brother Denis was ten. He still wore short pants, and got into fights over conkers with the boys at school. He still cried when Mam smacked him. He sometimes did odd-jobs for William Carty, the farmer who lived near us, but I couldn't imagine him moving away from home and having a real job.

The girl smiled at me. 'I'm Maggie,' she said. 'I'm the laundry maid. What's your name?'

'I'm Lily,' I said. 'Maggie is a pretty name.'

'It is,' she said. 'It's not really my name though.'

'But you said ...'

'My real name is Agnes, but one of the kitchen maids is called that, and she was here first, so Mrs Bailey says I have to be called Maggie.'

I could hardly believe what she was saying. 'She just took your name – the one your mam and dad chose for you?'

She nodded.

'She can't do that,' I said.

'Who can't do what, Lily?' asked Mrs Bailey.

I could feel my cheeks going bright red. Was I going to lose my job on my very first day?

'I was only.......I thought.....you see..........'

But just then the cook came in and started to talk to Mrs Bailey about the next day's menu, and I was saved.

'It doesn't sound fair to me,' I whispered to the girl next to me. 'I'll call you Agnes if you like.'

'That's nice of you, Lily,' she said, smiling. 'But it's all right. Having two names would be very complicated, and I'm used to being Maggie now.'

I smiled back at her. I was glad she was happy, but I couldn't help thinking – what if there was another Lily at Lissadell? What if I had to change the name I'd had for all my life? Would I ever be able to get over the unfairness of that?

* * *

We were all given a fine meal of meat and potatoes. I finished my food quickly, and picked up my plate to lick it – then I noticed that everyone was staring at me. I turned the plate around in my hands, pretending I was examining it. 'I've never seen a plate like this before,' I said. 'Such lovely stripes.'

After the meat and potatoes, there was dessert, and an apple for everyone. The meal seemed to go on for ages. There was mountains of food, far more than we ever had at home, and there was lots of talk and laughter. I couldn't enjoy myself, though. I was surrounded by strangers, and everything was so new and frightening. I wished I was back at my own table in my own little kitchen, eating bread and potatoes with people I loved.

* * *

After that, time went very slowly. All the days seemed the same, with hours and hours of work that never

72

got any easier. In the mornings I often thought about Rose and Hanora. Were they at school yet? Was it playtime, and were they playing Pickey or skipping? Were they busy in the classroom, learning all the things I might never know? Was Rose the best at reading, now that I was gone? At sewing time, was Miss O'Brien praising Hanora's tiny stitches, and saying she was a little star? I wondered were my friends thinking of me at all.

I spent most of my time with Nellie, which wasn't any fun, as she still seemed to be angry with me all the time. I only saw Isabelle once or twice, and she was always rushing back to the nursery. Maggie was friendly, but except for mealtimes, we were never together. The days were very long and every night I cried myself to sleep.

* * *

It was the strangest thing. Sir Josslyn and Lady Mary

were the owners of the house, and I knew they slept under the same roof as me, but it was almost as if they were ghosts. I tidied their slept-in beds, folded their newspapers, and swept up crumbs from their meals. Sometimes I went into a room and got a faint scent of perfume or hair oil, but I never once actually saw them. Nellie and I were following them around, cleaning each room as they left it. Life at Lissadell seemed to be arranged so that we would never meet. It was almost as if Nellie and I were carrying some contagious disease and had to be avoided no matter what happened. It wasn't a nice feeling.

* * *

Thursday was Nellie's day off, and I thought I would curl up and die from jealousy as I crawled out of bed, wondering how I'd get everything done without her to help me. It was a cold morning, and all I could see was a tangle of red hair, her bright blue eyes, and her

pointy nose poking out from under her blanket.

'I suppose you're going to see your family today,' I said as I got dressed in my uniform. 'You must be so excited. You probably have lots of things saved up to talk to them about. I have so many things to tell my family, I think I'm going to burst from holding them all in.'

Nellie didn't answer me. That shouldn't have been a surprise. I've always been a chatterbox, and some-times, first thing in the morning, I forgot that Nellie wasn't like me.

Then I looked closer at her, and her eyes seemed all watery. Maybe she had yawned while I was strug-gling with my apron – or maybe she was crying? That didn't make any sense though. Nellie was too tough for tears, and besides, why would she be crying on her day off, of all days? I knew my day off was going to be the best day of my whole life.

'So what time will you be leaving?' I asked. 'Have you far to go?'

'I'm not going anywhere,' she snapped.

'But your family ...?'

'My family live too far away. I couldn't get there and back in a day.'

Nellie might be the meanest girl I'd ever met, but maybe it wasn't her fault. I couldn't imagine how I'd live if I didn't have a trip home to dream about. How would I cope with the endless fires, and the dusting and polishing that never seemed to be finished? How would I survive if I had nothing to look forward to?

'I'm sorry, Nellie,' I said. 'I hope you enjoy your rest anyway.'

I was trying to be nice, but I knew I sounded stupid. Me and my big mouth!

Chapter Seven

*A*fter what felt like a hundred years, Saturday came around at last. I woke up and saw Nellie getting dressed. I could have stayed in my cosy bed for another while if I wanted, but I was much too excited for that. I jumped out of bed like a March hare.

It was a lovely feeling, leaving my uniform in the press, and putting on my own familiar Sunday dress that Mam had made for me out of an old skirt that Molly Carty didn't want any more. Just wearing my own clothes made the day feel different and special.

Nellie watched me lacing up my boots, and I waited for her to say something mean. I nearly fainted away when she gave me a little smile and said, 'I hope you have a nice day with your family.'

I wanted to tell her that she was pretty when she smiled, that her freckly nose crinkled up, and her

eyes twinkled, but I knew she wouldn't like that. So I smiled back at her. 'Thank you,' I said. 'I'll see you later.'

Even though I had worked hard and earned my day off, I couldn't help feeling sorry for Nellie, who had nothing ahead of her except another long, boring day of scrubbing and cleaning.

* * *

I walked as fast as I could, but still the journey home seemed to take forever. Could the road actually have got longer during the week? As I hurried along, I didn't waste time on counting clouds or collecting shells or paddling. I just wanted to see my mam again and feel her arms around me.

When I finally saw my house in the distance, I felt happy, and then sad too, because I hadn't been there for so long. When I got to the door, I hesitated. For a second, I had a strange feeling that I didn't belong

there any more, as if I were a visitor from a fara-way land, who had to knock and ask permission to be allowed in.

But then the door flew open and Mam came out, followed by Winnie and Anne. Mam hugged me tight, and the familiar smell of her made me feel homesick, even though I was back in my own lovely home. The girls clung on to my skirt and Winnie started to cry.

'She's missed you, the little pet,' said Mam. 'We've all missed you, but she's been the worst of all.'

I picked Winnie up and twirled her around, the way she loved. 'No crying today,' I said. 'I'm going to be here for hours and hours, and in the end you'll be fed up of me, and hoping for me to go.'

'The boys are helping to pick stones in Carty's back field,' said Mam. 'They wanted to take the day off, but I told them you'll still be here when they get home. Am I right?'

I was supposed to be back at Lissadell in time for

supper. If the boys were late, I thought maybe I'd have to run half the way back. But I couldn't disappoint my brothers, so I smiled and nodded.

We went inside, and at first it was a bit awkward. Mam sat down at the hearth and folded her arms, which was very strange. Usually she spends the whole day running around, cooking and cleaning and tending the garden and caring for the little ones. The girls made things easier though. They climbed all over me, and then I remembered the presents I'd brought for them. First I gave them the shells, which they lined up on the floor, as if they were fine jewels. Next I pulled the cloth from my pocket, revealing the five tiny cakes I'd managed to save from my suppers during the week.

'There's one for everyone,' I said. 'Including you, Mam.'

The girls each grabbed a cake, and stuffed them into their mouths.

'I'll save mine for later,' said Mam. I felt sad. I knew

she'd hide it away, and give it to one of the little ones when I was gone.

'No, Mam,' I said. 'Eat it now, or I'll be offended.'

She picked up the smallest cake and took a little nibble. Then she took a second nibble and a third.

'That's like eating a little bit of heaven,' she said, as a slow smile spread over her tired face. I watched her, and for one second, the whole week away seemed worth it, so I could bring her that little bit of happiness.

After that, things were fine. I helped Mam with some jobs, and then we went for a walk up the road. I carried Winnie, and Anne skipped ahead of us, with her long hair flying out behind her in the wind.

The neighbours greeted me as if I'd been gone for years. Molly Carty was all excited when she saw me. She held tightly on to my arm, so I couldn't escape without answering all of her questions.

'Tell me about that Lissadell place, Lily,' she said. 'Is it as fancy as they say?'

'It's fancy all right,' I said.

'And is it true that every one of the family has a big feather bed to themselves?'

'They do,' I said. I wanted to tell her that I even had a whole bed to myself, but I knew Mam would give out to me for boasting.

'And have you met that Countess Markievicz woman?'

'No,' I said. 'She lives in Dublin, and only visits sometimes.'

'You know I've heard she's not even a proper Countess,' said Molly. 'They say her husband made up the title to impress his friends.'

'She's more a Countess than you or I will ever be, Molly,' said Mam, and Molly gave her a sour look.

'I could tell you stories about that woman,' said Molly. 'And they'd make your hair stand on end. I heard that one time in Paris she—'

Now I was very interested, but Mam nudged Molly. 'Not in front of the children,' she said.

I think Molly's a bit afraid of Mam, so I'll probably never know the end of the Paris story.

'Well, it won't hurt the children to hear how that
woman carries on in Dublin,' said Molly. 'She says
she's working for the people, but she traipses off to
meetings all dressed up in velvet ball gowns, with dia-
monds around her neck. She's the talk of the town,
she is – always looking for attention.'

I know Molly was trying to badmouth the Countess, and make me think less of her, but it wasn't
working. The Countess sounded like a very interesting woman, and I loved to think that she grew up in
the house where I worked. She had actually walked
along the corridors I swept, and slept in the beds I
turned over and aired. I had seen the window where
she scratched her name one wet afternoon when she
was bored. I couldn't help feeling excited that one
day I might actually see her in real life. I was ready to
hear more stories, but Mam hates gossip, and I knew
we'd have to go.

'We need to move on,' said Mam, pulling me away from Molly. 'The day will be gone before we know it.' And the thought of my special day coming to an end made me sad as we walked back home.

* * *

Later, Mam and I made dinner together, and though the food was plain and simple, I enjoyed the meal more than any I'd had in my week in Lissadell.

After dinner, Mam said she had loads of darning to do, so she sat down and began to work. I knew she was only making an excuse so we could have some quiet time together – but I didn't tell her that. Anne can't sit still for five minutes, so I was glad when she begged to go next door to play with their new litter of kittens. I wanted to have a proper chat with Mam before the boys came home.

Winnie climbed onto my lap, put her thumb in her mouth, and used her other hand to play with my

curls. Within seconds she was asleep. I wanted that moment to last forever and ever, with my little sister warm in my arms, and my lovely mam sitting across from me, listening as if my stories were the best stories she'd ever heard in her whole life.

'And how are things in the Big House, Lily?' asked Mam. 'Are you doing everything they tell you? You're not being skittish? Is the work hard? Are they good to you?'

So I told her all about my new life. Mam is a great listener, and I know she missed my company when I was gone, so I made it all sound funny, even the endless sweeping and dusting, and the blackleading of the grates that left my fingers stained and sore.

I didn't tell her that for much of the time I was afraid of doing or saying something wrong. I didn't tell her that for much of the time I was lonely, and almost ready to cry.

'And have you made any friends?' she asked.

I told her about Isabelle, and Maggie and how nice

they were to me, and I could see that made her happy.

'And then there's Nellie,' I said.

'Is she your friend too?'

'I wouldn't say that. We sleep in the same room, and we work together every day, but I don't think she's my friend.'

'Why not?'

'I'm not really sure. Mostly she's grumpy and barely talks to me, so I decide I hate her, and then she surprises me and gets all chatty and I decide I like her again, and then she's mean and – I don't know, Mam. It's hard when I don't know if she's nice or not.'

Mam put down her needle and patted my hand.

'Oh dear. That does sound a bit confusing, but you know what they say – you shouldn't judge someone until you've walked a mile in their shoes.'

'I'd never walk a mile, or even one single step in Nellie's shoes. She'd *murder* me if she saw me touching anything of hers.'

Mam laughed. 'You know exactly what I mean.

Just give her a chance, and who knows – maybe one day this Nellie girl will be your very best friend.'

* * *

The afternoon passed in a flash, and soon I could hear my brothers outside, scuffling as always, as they kicked a stone along the track ahead of them. They burst through the door, and stood shyly next to me. I smiled at their sweet dirty faces, and their unusual silence. I gave them their cakes, which they ate at once, all in one bite.

'Is the house massive?' asked Jimmy, wiping a crumb from his face with a very dirty hand. 'And is it all fancy? And do you have to bow when you're talking to the rich people? And do they have sweets and chocolate for breakfast?'

I answered all of his questions, and then Denis piped up. 'A boy at school said they have a motor car, but that couldn't be true, could it?'

'Actually that boy was right,' I said. 'The Gore-Booths *do* have a motor car. It's called a Wolseley Siddeley.'

I knew this because I'd heard the nice driver, Albert, telling one of the stable boys all about it. I don't understand why he laughed when the boy said that motor cars would never catch on, and that people would always need horses for getting around.

'Where do they go in the car?' asked Jimmy.

'I heard someone say they go on holidays to Bundoran,' I said. 'And they go away on fishing trips.'

'If I owned a house like Lissadell,' said Mam with a big sigh. 'I wouldn't leave it for anyone. I'd sit in my fancy living room with my feet on a cushion and never wish for another thing in my whole life.'

'Have you seen the car with your own two eyes?' asked Denis.

I nodded. I had actually seen it through the window once when I was shaking out Lady Mary's eiderdown.

'What's it like?' he asked.

'It's dark blue and huge and shiny, and it makes a lot of noise,' I said.

Denis was looking at me with more respect than ever before.

'Did you get a drive in it?' asked Jimmy.

Mam laughed. 'There's a thought!' she said. 'People like us won't ever be going around in cars. It's a good day for us when a farmer gives us a lift in a pony and trap.'

Jimmy looked embarrassed, and I felt sorry for him. When you're a child, it's never nice to have grown-ups laughing at you.

'I'd love to get a drive in it, Jimmy,' I said. 'But I don't expect I'll ever be in a motor car. Mam's right – they will always be only for rich people.'

Soon after that, Hanora and Rose came to visit. It was strange at first. I thought they might have changed but they were just the same – I felt different though. The three of us sat on the bench outside our

house, like we had a hundred times before. Hanora
and Rose talked about what happened at school that
week. They mentioned history and sums and the new
skipping game they played during lunch break. I listened and smiled but it all seemed foreign – as if my
two old friends were living in a world that I had left
behind forever.

Soon they had to go home to help their mams and
dads, and when they left, Mam said it was time for
me to go back to Lissadell.

'Let me make you up a small parcel of food for the
journey,' she said when I was ready to leave.

'I'm so full after the dinner,' I said. 'I don't think I
could eat another bite.'

I was really quite hungry, but Mam and the little
ones didn't have much to spare, and I knew there
were all kinds of treats waiting for me in the servants'
hall. So I kissed everyone goodbye, and set off on my
long walk.

Chapter Eight

It was a strange feeling, walking along the shore at Lissadell again, and coming around the bend and seeing the Big House between the trees. Only a week had passed since my first day, but already everything was different. I knew which gate to walk through and where to find the servants' tunnel. I knew exactly how Lady Mary liked her towels folded. I knew my place at the big servants' table and I knew not to pull out my chair until Butler Kilgallon and Mrs Bailey were seated. It's funny how easily you get used to new things

* * *

Morning came much too quickly. I'd been dreaming I was at home, cuddled up in bed, telling stories

to Winnie and Anne, looking forward to a day at school. I wasn't happy when Nellie shook my arm and I remembered I was at Lissadell, and my school-days were over.

The morning passed quickly, and after lunch, Mrs Bailey told me to dust and sweep the big staircase. Nellie and I and the other servants always used the back stairs, so I'd never gone up the main one, which was very fancy. The steps were made of black stone that was polished so much I could nearly see my face in it. The pillars were decorated with swirls and flowers, and halfway up each one was a lovely golden bird with its wings spread out. It was so beautiful! I wished I was good at drawing so I could do a picture to show to my mam – she loves pretty things – and doesn't have many of them in her life.

I dusted everything very carefully and then I went back to the top of the stairs and began to sweep. I was walking backwards, sweeping slowly and being careful not to raise up all the dust, as Mrs Bailey had

warned me – and then I bumped into someone! I guessed it was probably Nellie coming to see if I was doing my job properly. I was ready for her to shout at me, and tell me how useless I was, when I heard a soft voice. When I turned around and saw a lady, I nearly collapsed on the spot.

'Oh, Madam, Miss, My Lady, I'm ever so sorry,' I said. 'I was concentrating on the sweeping and I wasn't looking and I should have been looking and it's all my fault, and did I hurt you, and ...?'

I stopped talking. Too late, I remembered that I wasn't supposed to say a word to the family unless they spoke to me first.

Would I lose my job for this?

Would I have to go home to Mam and tell her that my big mouth had got me into trouble again?

Would I get sent to some horrible house where the servants got beaten and were half-starved?

But the woman was smiling. 'You can call me Lady Mary,' she said, in her beautiful voice. 'You must be

the new housemaid – Lily, isn't it?'

I nodded as I squashed myself up against the wall and tried to look small. If I could, I would have disappeared altogether.

'It's nice to meet you, Lily,' she said. 'I hope everyone is treating you well?'

I nodded again.

'That's good. I hope you will be very happy here,' she said, and then she walked on up the stairs. My heart was thumping so hard I felt it was going to jump right out of my chest and go bouncing all the way down the shiny stone steps. A few minutes later, all that remained was the smell of Lady Mary's perfume, and I wondered if she'd been a vision rather than a real person.

Over the next few weeks, I saw Lady Mary twice again, and she smiled at me, but she never said another word. Once I saw Sir Josslyn, but he didn't look in my direction, and I don't think he even noticed that I was there, scrubbing his rug on his landing in his

house on this huge big estate. Every now and then I saw the little ones with Isabelle or one of the other nurses. The babies looked so sweet, all dressed up in satin and lace, and seeing them made me miss my own dear sisters. It seemed strange though – all of us, family and servants, were living in the same house, breathing the same air, but we were always apart. It reminded me of the farm near our village, where the sheep and the pigs were kept in separate fields, with a thick stone wall between them. Sometimes it didn't make any sense to me at all.

* * *

One morning I went into a small room off the kitchen and saw Harry, one of the footmen ironing the newspapers. I leaned across to read the headlines and he smiled. 'Don't bother looking, Lily,' he said. 'The world is changing, but not fast enough for me. The papers always have the same old news.'

'So what news is there today?'

'The Lockout's still going on, I'm afraid.'

'I've heard people talking about the Lockout,' I said. 'But I don't really understand what it is. Could you tell me who has been locked out – and why?'

Most of the senior servants still scared me, and I'd never dare to ask them anything. Harry was nice, though, and I knew he wouldn't laugh at me.

'It's been going on since August,' he said. 'The big employers locked out all the workers who wouldn't resign from their union, and now there's thousands out of work.'

'That's terrible.'

'You can say that again. We're lucky down here in the country, but there's people in Dublin who are nearly starved to death – even little children.'

'And isn't anyone doing anything to help them?'

Harry looked over his shoulder, and when he spoke again, it was almost in a whisper.

'The Countess has done a lot to help.'

'How?'

'I could tell you a hundred good things she's done, but I've got work to do. Sir Josslyn will be waiting for these newspapers.'

'Please,' I said. 'Just tell me a few things about her. No one around here ever wants to talk about the Countess – and that makes her seem so mysterious and interesting.'

'She's an interesting woman, all right. Lately she's been selling her jewellery to raise money for people who are hungry. And she's helped to set up a soup kitchen, so the children will have something warm in their bellies. I hear she goes down to the basement of Liberty Hall herself, puts a sack over her fine dress to protect it, and peels potatoes with the other women.'

'She sounds like a very kind lady to me,' I said. 'Sir Josslyn and Lady Mary should be proud of her.'

He smiled. 'Maybe they are – in their own way. Thing is, some people think the Countess isn't very ladylike – what she does embarrasses them. It's not

what they expect from a woman of her station.'

'What *do* they expect of a woman like her? Why can't she—?'

I was enjoying the conversation, and trying to make it go on longer, but Harry interrupted me.

'Got to go,' he said. 'These papers should have been in the breakfast room ten minutes ago.'

I watched as he took the papers and ran up the back stairs. I gave a big sigh. Countess Markievicz! When was I going to see this exotic lady?

* * *

Soon every working day began to feel like the one before. Isabelle said there were fifty-eight fireplaces in Lissadell, and some days it felt as if I had cleaned and lit every one ten times over. I couldn't count how many ornaments I had dusted or floors I had swept.

Most of the rooms downstairs had shelves full of books. At first I used to hope that maybe Lady Mary

would let me take one to my room so I could read at night, but soon I realised that was a foolish thought. When bedtime came, I was always half-dead from tiredness, and I only had time for a quick prayer in my head before falling fast asleep.

Nellie and I spent most of every day together and she was nearly always grumpy and mean. Her rare smiles were like treats, that vanished before I had time to enjoy them properly.

I'd spend days looking forward to my day off, and then it would come and be over in a flash, and I'd have six more long days of work ahead of me.

I had a warm bed and plenty to eat, but I was often sad. I was often lonely.

I never had any fun.

And then one day something strange happened.

Chapter Nine

It was evening time, and Nellie and I went upstairs to prepare the bedrooms for the night. By now I could almost do this in my sleep, so my mind was on my own bed and how badly I wanted to be there. Nellie had been coughing for hours the night before, and I had barely managed to sleep a wink.

'Lady Georgina and Miss Maeve are here,' said Nellie. 'So that means two extra rooms for us to prepare.'

'What are they like?' I asked.

'Lady Georgina is a real angel down from Heaven,' said Nellie. 'Back in the famine days, she did so much for the poor people.'

'Like what?' I asked. Isabelle had told me something about this already, but I didn't care – I hoped that if I kept Nellie talking about the family, she

might forget to be mean to me.

'Lady Georgina and Miss Constance and Master Josslyn and Miss Eva set up a stall and gave food to anyone who was hungry. Imagine that – their own food, and they gave it over with their own hands! There's not many did that.'

Nellie was standing with her two hands pressed together, and there was a strange sparkle in her bright blue eyes.

'And once, when Lady Georgina heard that some people had no beds to sleep on, she sent straw from her own sheds down to the cottages, to give the people some little bit of comfort in their hard, hungry days.'

'That was kind of her,' I said. 'And what about Miss Maeve? What's she like?'

For a minute, Nellie didn't say anything. 'Poor Miss Maeve,' she said in the end. 'Sometimes I feel sorry for her. Her father is always vanishing away to that foreign country he comes from, and her mother is off in Dublin, getting involved in things no woman

should ever bother with. But then I say to myself, Nellie, why are you feeling sorry for Miss Maeve, when she lives in a fine house, and sleeps in a fat feather bed every night?'

'But what's she *like*?' I asked again.

Nellie ignored my question. 'Hurry up,' she said. 'Get hot bottles for all the beds and extra for Lady Georgina – she feels the cold more than most.'

I put hot bottles in all the beds, and I was making my way out of Miss Maeve's room, when I saw a girl coming towards me. She was taller than me, but it was hard to guess her age. She had huge eyes and long wavy hair down to her waist, like a princess in a storybook. She was dressed for dinner in a beautiful pale pink dress with pearls on the sleeves. By now I had learned what to do, so I stood to the side and looked down at the floor, so she could pass me.

I was still looking at the floor, when she stopped next to me.

I kept my eyes down and concentrated on her feet.

She was wearing the most gorgeous shoes I had ever seen.

'I don't bite, you know.'

I looked up at her, with no idea what to say.

'I haven't seen you before, have I?' she said. 'My name is Maeve, what's yours?'

'I'm Lily,' I whispered.

'I was named after Maeve of Connacht,' she said. 'She was a brave warrior queen. If you look out the window of my bedroom you can see her burial mound at Knocknarea.'

And then the words popped out of my mouth. 'I was named after my daddy's mam. She wasn't a queen, but she was the most beautiful woman in the whole parish and she could sing like a lark. If you go to the churchyard near my house, you can see where she's buried.'

'My mother is Countess Markievicz, and she is in Dublin fighting for the rights of women and poor people. One day she will be famous all over Ireland.'

Maeve and I seemed to be playing some kind of game, and even though I was happy to play, I knew this was a game I could never win. I remembered all the warnings Nellie and Mam had given me, but I couldn't stay quiet.

'My mother is Josephine Mary Brennan,' I said. 'And she is at home minding my little brothers and sisters. One day she will be famous for keeping our family from starving in very hard times.'

At first Maeve didn't answer, and I was afraid I had gone too far. If this was a game, she was definitely making the rules. Then she laughed out loud.

'You're very funny, Lily,' she said. 'Did you know that?'

I liked being funny, it reminded me of the days when I was one of the most popular girls at school, when I could make Hanora and Rose and every-one else laugh, without even trying. Sometimes the Master tried to look cross when I was being skittish, but his smile always won out in the end. This

was different though. I didn't like this rich girl saying such things out loud in the corridor of this fine house, where I could get into trouble for even talking to her. I looked over my shoulder, afraid of being seen. If Nellie came along, or Mrs Bailey, or even Butler Kilgallon ...

'What's wrong?' asked Maeve.

I'm really afraid that someone might see me, and I'll get into lots of trouble with Mrs Bailey, and might actually lose my job – and that's not fair, when I was only trying to be funny.

Even if I could find the words to explain all this to Maeve, would a rich girl like her ever understand? What did she know about having a job, and being afraid of losing it? When was her family ever depending on her to make money so they could eat? Life was much easier when I was at school with my friends and no one was supposed to be better than anyone else.

But Maeve surprised me. 'I understand,' she said. 'Here, come into my room.'

She opened the door, and I had no choice but to follow her inside. She sat on the bed and patted the space beside her. 'Sit down,' she said.

I had been in that room many times before. I'd shaken the eiderdowns, and swept the floors and dusted everything. I had never, ever dared to sit down on the bed.

'I think I'd prefer to stand,' I said. I was still afraid, still looking at the door. This really wasn't fair. I had to do what Maeve said, but soon Nellie would come looking for me. If I got caught, I'd be the one in trouble, not this pretty girl in the fancy pink dress.

'I think I'd better go back downstairs,' I said. 'I have jobs to do.'

'If someone comes, you can say you are doing a job in here for me.'

'But there's nothing to do here,' I said, looking around the room. I had done my work well, and everything was clean and in its place.

Maeve stood up and ran to the mantelpiece. She

grabbed a large china ornament and threw it to the floor, where it broke into a thousand pieces. I jumped. I had never seen anyone do anything like that before.

'There's something to do now,' she said.

'But...'

'Don't worry, Lily,' she said. 'This house is full of ornaments and I've always hated that one. Some boring old poet gave it to my mother ages ago.'

'But it's...'

'Don't worry. No one will care. Well, maybe my grandmother, Gaga, will, but she's very old-fashioned – and I won't tell her if you don't.'

I walked over and bent to pick up the biggest pieces, but she pulled me back.

'Leave it,' she said. 'I can clean up later. It's just there in case of emergencies.'

I went over and fixed the bed where she had wrinkled it by sitting down. She went back and sat down and messed it up again. I don't think she was being mean – I think she had no idea what it was like to

have to tidy up after herself or anyone else.

I stood near the fireplace with my hands clasped behind my back. I was confused. I wanted to leave, but I also wanted to stay and get to know this girl better.

Now she was staring at me.

'Do you know you have a very interesting face?' she said.

I had no idea what to say to that so I said nothing.

Maeve got up from the bed, and I had to stop myself from going over and fixing it again. She walked around me, staring at my face all the time. I thought she was being a bit rude – you'd expect a rich girl like her to have better manners.

'Has anyone ever painted your portrait?' she asked.

I laughed, but she didn't laugh with me, and I realised she hadn't been joking.

'Last year my little sister, Anne, found some chalk, and she drew a picture of me on the wall of our house,' I said. 'I had a big head and no body and long

legs like sticks, and Mam gave my sister a slap for ruining the wall.'

'I would like to paint your portrait,' said Maeve when she finally stopped laughing.

Now it was my time to stare at her. I didn't know this girl very well, but I could see that she was being perfectly serious.

'My parents are very famous artists,' she said. 'My mother trained in Paris and London, you know. I think I may have inherited their talent. They will be so proud of me when they see I can paint a good portrait. Sometimes I try to paint my cousins, but they don't have interesting faces like yours – and they are not very good at sitting still. Yes, I have made up my mind – you would be a very good subject. What do you think about that?'

I could feel my face going red. 'Em…it's very nice of you… thank you… but I'm not sure if…'

'It would be only an hour or two a day.'

'But, Miss Maeve, I don't have time for that – I

have to work.'

'Please call me Maeve,' she said. 'And don't worry, I think I could arrange it with Mrs Bailey and Mr Kilgallon – they always do what I say. And besides, my father once painted Mr Kilgallon, and my mother did a lovely drawing of a servant girl just like you, so I'm merely following a family tradition.'

Now I didn't know what to do. This was all very strange and new. Sitting in Maeve's room being painted sounded like much more fun than scrubbing floors, but what would the other servants say? Nellie would go mad – and while I didn't mind the idea of that, I knew she would make me suffer for it later.

Just thinking about Nellie must have worked some evil magic, because right then I heard her voice.

'Lily, where have you got to? There's still lots of work to do. Where are you?'

'I've got to go,' I whispered, as I ran to the door in a panic.

Maeve lay back on the bed with her hands behind

her head. 'See you soon,' she said, as I closed the door behind me.

Nellie was coming along the corridor, and she did not look happy.

'Were you idling in Miss Maeve's room?' she said. 'I should go right to Mrs Bailey and complain you.'

'Miss Maeve is in her room,' I said. 'And she needed me to tidy up something she had broken. She especially asked me to stay and give her a hand.'

Nellie looked doubtful, but even she wouldn't dare go into Maeve's room to see if I was telling the truth. I didn't know how much of a mess I had got myself into, but it was almost worth it to see the look of jealousy on Nellie's face.

Chapter Ten

The next morning, Nellie and I were supposed to polish the silver, but first Mrs Bailey asked me to carry a bundle of clean towels upstairs to the nursery. I wondered how a few small babies could use so many towels. I didn't mind though – I might meet Isabelle, and have a minute for a quick chat.

At the bottom of the back stairs, I bumped into Nellie.

'Where are you going with those?'

She looked suspiciously at the bundle of towels, almost as if I were going to steal them away and trade them for a bar of gold.

'I'm bringing them to—'

Before I could finish the sentence, I was interrupted by a familiar voice. 'Lily, there you are.'

Maeve was coming down the back stairs, which

was very strange, as the family always used the big staircase. Automatically, Nellie and I stepped aside, and stood against the wall.

'I've been looking for you, Lily,' said Maeve.

'Good morning, Miss Maeve,' I said.

'Didn't I tell you to call me Maeve?'

Nellie's mouth opened wide, but no sound came out.

'I have found a solution to our little problem,' said Maeve.

Nellie's mouth opened even wider. The thought of Maeve and I sharing anything, even a problem, must have been hard for her to bear.

Since I didn't say anything, Maeve went on talking.

'You said you have a lot of work to do every day, Lily?'

'Yes, Miss ... I mean yes ... Maeve.'

'But you have a whole day off every week?'

'Yes,' I said again, not liking where this conversation was going.

'And when is your day off?'

'Saturday,' I said quietly.

Maeve clapped her hands. 'Perfect. Gaga and I are leaving this morning, but I will ask Uncle Joss to pick me up his motor car on Saturday and we can get started on the portrait of you.'

I could feel tears coming to my eyes. For Maeve, every day was a day off, so how could she imagine how precious my Saturdays were to me?

What would Mam do if I didn't come to see her?

Would she worry that I was sick?

Would the girls cry if I wasn't there to play with them and tell them stories?

Would the boys miss me helping with their reading and writing?

Would Hanora and Rose think I'd forgotten all about them?

What would I do if I had to go two whole weeks without seeing my family?

Maeve was still talking. 'It will probably be about

twelve o'clock by the time I get here. My paints are still in the day nursery, but I don't think we should work there – the children can be frightfully annoying. We can work in my bedroom, or maybe one of the studies – anyway, I'll think about that and set up the paints later. Mother will be so proud of me when she hears that I have taken up painting again. She says....'

'But that's not fair.'

That's what I was thinking, but I hadn't said a word. Or had I?

Then I saw that, beside me, Nellie had gone red and clamped a hand over her mouth. Nellie had said the words! For a minute there was silence. I think we were all a bit shocked by what had happened.

'What do you mean, Nellie?'

Maeve had spoken quietly, and it was hard to tell if she was angry, or just asking because she didn't understand.

Nellie looked terrified, and I felt sorry for her. She

spent her days telling me about all the rules I had to follow, and now she had broken one of the most important ones – she had been rude to a member of the family.

Maeve was staring at her. I suppose ignoring a member of the family was nearly as bad as being rude to them.

'Begging your pardon, Miss Maeve,' whispered Nellie. 'I'm sorry if I'm speaking out of turn, but, on her day off, Lily goes to see her family – and family is important, and that's why it's not fair if Lily has to stay here and get painted.'

At first Maeve didn't reply, and that made me scared. She was best friends with Mrs Bailey, and maybe she was planning to get Nellie and me sacked! Maybe she didn't even need to involve Mrs Bailey – maybe she could just say the word and Nellie and I would have to go and pack up our belongings and leave. Next to me, I could feel Nellie shaking.

But then Maeve shrugged. 'Oh, all right,' she said.

'I didn't think about that. We'll just have to do it on a working day. Don't you worry, Lily – I'll make all the arrangements and I'll let you know when I'm back. Bye.'

And she waved at us both and walked on down the stairs.

'Thank you so much, Nellie,' I said. 'You have saved my life. I'd die if I couldn't go to see my family. And I'm sorry your family lives so far away – do you miss them an awful lot?'

But instead of answering my question, Nellie snapped at me.

'You'll get in trouble for being too familiar with Miss Maeve,' she said, sounding like her usual self. 'Letting her paint you – I've never heard the like of it. Who do you think you are, Miss Hoity Toity? Now bring those towels wherever you are supposed to and then come back – the silver won't polish itself you know.'

Isabelle met me at the door of the nursery. It was lovely to see her friendly, smiling face.

'Lily,' she said. 'How are you? How are you settling in?'

'I think I'm settling in all right,' I said. 'Sometimes I miss my family, but mostly it's not too bad. Mrs Bailey said I'm a good worker, so I'm happy about that.'

'I wish I could see you more, but I have to spend most of my time up here with the little ones. They are very sweet, but they keep me on my toes.'

I couldn't help feeling a bit jealous. Spending time playing with those adorable children sounded nicer than the way I spent my days.

'Isabelle,' I said. 'I wonder – do you think I could be a children's maid? I've got four brothers and sisters at home – so I'm used to taking care of little ones.'

'That would be very nice. You and I could have

good times, chatting and telling stories and playing games with the little ones.'

'So maybe...?'

She shook her head. 'I don't think so. Around here, once you've been trained for one job, that's the job you keep on doing.'

'But when I started here, Mrs Bailey said I wouldn't be an under-housemaid forever.'

'She was right. If you work hard, maybe one day you'll be a housemaid, and in many years time your dreams might come true and you could even be made housekeeper.'

I wasn't sure that my wildest dream was to be a housekeeper. Mrs Bailey didn't have any family, and she spent her whole life in the servants' quarters in Lissadell. (Though I did envy Mrs Bailey her own office, and her little sitting room with its own fire-place and an armchair where she had tea and cakes every evening.)

'And what about you, Isabelle?' I asked. 'What do

you dream of?'

'I like being a children's maid, but I hope that one day I'll be a children's nurse. I'll get more pay, and I'll be able to boss the maids around – I'd like that.'

I laughed. I knew Isabelle was much too nice to boss anyone around.

'Come with me while I put away these towels,' said Isabelle. 'But be quiet. The little ones are still sleeping.'

I followed her into the nursery, and I could hardly believe my eyes. It was like something from a picture book. Everything seemed to be made of satin or lace or velvet. There were shelves full of toys and stuffed animals and books. On a chair was the most beautiful doll I had ever seen. She was dressed all in cream-coloured lace. She had long curly black hair and she had the sweetest face you could imagine.

'Could I touch her?' I whispered.

'Of course,' said Isabelle, picking up the doll and passing her to me. 'Miss Bridget has lots of dolls,

though she's too small to play with them anyway.'

I held the doll in my arms, and rocked her for a minute, thinking of my own dear Winnie and Anne at home, who had never owned a doll, and didn't even know to dream of one. Then I carefully placed the doll back on the chair, and went back out to the corridor.

'See you soon, Lily,' said Isabelle.

'Can I tell you something before I go?' I asked.

'Of course,' she said quickly. 'Is there something wrong?'

'No ... not really ... well maybe. I think you're my friend... and ...'

Isabelle gave me a warm smile. 'I am your friend,' she said. 'And you can tell me anything.'

So I told her about Miss Maeve's plan to paint a portrait of me.

'Oh dear,' she said when I was finished. 'You must be careful, Lily. No one likes it when we get above our station.'

'But what am I supposed to do? None of this is my fault – I wasn't forward in any way. Miss Maeve is very bossy, and if she tells me I have to sit down and let her paint me, I can't say no. I can't run away and hide under the stairs or stand in the gallery and pretend to be a statue, can I?'

'That's true,' said Isabelle, giggling. 'Maybe if you stay out of her way for a while she'll forget all about you?'

'Thank you, but how can I do that? I go where I'm told, and Maeve goes wherever she wants. Even in a big house like this, if she wants to find me, she'll find me.'

'That's true. It's a problem all right – and I'm sorry I can't think of a solution for you.'

I was disappointed that Isabelle hadn't come up with any useful ideas, but simply talking about my problem had helped a little bit.

'I'd better go,' I said. 'Nellie will be wondering where I've got to.'

'Is Nellie being kind to you?'

'That's a hard question. Sometimes she's nice and sometimes she's mean, so I never know what to expect. This morning she did a very kind thing for me, but five minutes later she was snapping at me again.'

'That sounds like Nellie.'

'I try not to make her angry, but it doesn't take much to set her off.'

'I'm sorry to hear that, and it must be hard for you, being with her all day, but maybe ... it isn't her fault.'

'Well it's not my fault!' I said quickly. 'I'm trying my very hardest to be the perfect housemaid, and I bite my tongue a hundred times a day when Nellie says mean things to me.'

'Oh, I'm not blaming you. It's just that ... considering where Nellie came from ...'

'What do you mean?'

'She came from the workhouse – didn't you know?'

'The workhouse!'

Just saying the word brought a chill to my bones. At home in the village, talk of the workhouse could make big grown-up men go pale and scared-looking. Children ran away crying whenever it was mentioned. I had never seen a workhouse, but that didn't stop me from being terrified of the idea.

'As far as I know she wasn't much more than a baby when she was sent there,' said Isabelle.

'There's not many get out of the workhouse?' I said. 'How did she get here to Lissadell?'

'Lady Mary rescued her last year,' said Isabelle. 'I was there when she arrived – and she was a sight, I can tell you.'

'The poor girl.'

'She was skin and bone, her face was covered with sores and her hair was matted and filthy. I felt sorry for her, but I wouldn't stand too close to her either – she stank like anything – and she probably had lice. When she was bathing, one of the stable lads had to take her ragged clothes outside and burn them.'

'That's so sad.'

'It is. After her bath, Lady Mary brought her a plate of food, and Nellie ate it with her fingers, she was so hungry.'

I thought of the Nellie I knew, who tried to speak in a fancy voice, and who kept herself so clean and tidy.

'What happened next?' I asked.

'Lady Mary insisted that she stay in bed for a whole week, and she brought her meals herself – all the best butter and cream and meat. And slowly, Nellie got better, until she became the girl you know now.'

'And what about her family? Are they still in the workhouse?'

'Who knows? They could be there, or they could be dead. I'd like to ask Nellie – but, to be honest, I'm a little bit afraid of her.'

I felt sick when I thought of all the times I had prattled to Nellie about Mam and the little ones at home, and the fun we had, and the games we played

and the stories we shared.

How many times had I told Nellie that sometimes we were hungry at home, even though Mam always made sure we had something warm to eat in the morning, and before bed?

How many times had I told Nellie I was sad to have no daddy, when she might have no daddy or mam or family of any kind at all?

'Poor Nellie,' I whispered. 'I thought she was being mean, but maybe I was the mean one.'

* * *

It was bedtime before Nellie and I were on our own together. As usual, she jumped into bed quickly, and only grunted when I said goodnight. I felt awkward. I had so much to say to her, but I couldn't find the words.

Maybe she'd be offended if she thought I knew about the workhouse. She was only a baby when she

went there, so it wasn't her fault or anything. Where I lived, though, that didn't matter. Being in the workhouse was seen as a bit shameful, even though the shame should have been on the people who ran those terrible places.

So in the end I just made my voice as warm as possible when I said, 'Thank you again for standing up for me with Miss Maeve. I'll tell my mam what you did, and I know she will be very grateful too.'

'You're welcome,' whispered Nellie. 'Family is important.'

I was feeling happy when she followed this with a snappy, 'Now go to sleep. Your chattering is giving me a headache!'

Chapter Eleven

Over the next few days, part of me dreaded meeting Maeve again. I could see already that she was a determined kind of girl, so I knew she would come looking for me. But even if she sorted everything out with Mrs Bailey, I couldn't imagine the other servants being happy about me lazing about in Maeve's room while they continued with their work. It might be nice to spend time with Maeve, but if that made everyone downstairs hate me, my life would not be easy.

On the other hand, part of me wanted to know Maeve better. My life in Lissadell was busy, with every minute accounted for, but it was very boring. Except for Saturdays, every day was pretty much the same, and I longed for some excitement. Maeve was a young girl, just like me, but our lives were so differ-

ent. I wanted to know what she believed in, what she was afraid of, what was important to her. I wondered if we could be friends.

* * *

A few days later I was putting fresh flowers into the drawing room vases when I saw Sir Josslyn's motor car driving into the *porte cochere*. I peeped out the door and soon I saw Maeve and her Gaga coming into the front hall. Lady Georgina looked as if she were dressed for a ball, in a fine silk gown and a hat with long feathers on it. Maeve was wearing a very strange garment over her dress and she was carrying an easel and a giant notebook.

I went back to my work and five minutes later she found me. 'I'll do that,' she said, grabbing the last bunch of flowers and shoving them into a vase any old way. 'Come on, I'd like to get started while the morning light is good.'

'But I still have to.....'

'It's all arranged. Mrs Bailey is happy for you to come with me – well maybe not exactly happy, but she's allowing it in any case, which is just as good.'

'Maybe just as good for you,' I whispered.

Unfortunately, Maeve's hearing was very good.

'Don't worry, Lily,' she said. 'Truly, as long as you are with me, everything will be fine. I won't let anything happen to you, I promise.'

I nodded, hoping very much that she was right.

She noticed me staring at her strange clothes. 'Do you like my artist's smock?' she asked. 'I had it sent from Dublin. My mother used to have one just like it. I'm taking this portrait very seriously you know – and I hope you are too.'

I put my hand over my mouth to hide my smile. Maeve could have saved herself a lot of trouble and expense, as the 'artist's smock' looked very much like the overall the scullery maid used when she was scrubbing the kitchen floor.

'Now you go away down to your room and change,' she said. 'And I'll see you in my bedroom in a few minutes.'

'Change?'

'Yes. I know my mother drew a servant in uniform, but that's not what I have in mind for this portrait. You need to put on something else. Perhaps a dress in pink, or pale blue – with pearls or a bit of lace at the neck? Do you have something like that? It will be a challenge to paint lace, but if I don't push myself, how will I ever improve?'

She had to be joking. Did she have any idea how I lived my life? Did she think I had a different dress for every day, like she had? Or maybe even different ones for breakfast, dinner and tea? All I had was my uniform and two dresses – one grey and one brown, and I had never in my whole life owned anything with lace on it.

'I don't ...'

Maeve was decent enough to go red.

'Oh, I see,' she said. 'That was silly of me. Well never mind. Just come along with me and we will figure something out.'

I followed her – it was strange to be on the main stairs without my sweeping brush and duster. When we got to Maeve's room I was happy when she closed the door behind us – the fewer people who saw this, the better, as far as I was concerned.

Maeve already had the easel set up by the window, with her paints on a table nearby. She pulled over a chair, and told me to sit down and then she looked at me for a long time.

'No,' she said in the end. 'I'm afraid that uniform won't do at all. I think some of my old dresses are still in the wardrobe. Let's have a look.'

I followed her into the dressing room, and watched as she flung the wardrobe doors open. The racks were filled with dresses in every colour of the rainbow.

'I've outgrown all of these,' she said. 'But luckily you're a bit smaller than me, so they should fit you

perfectly. Which one do you like?'

I was speechless. They were all so beautiful! I hardly dared to touch them, and the thought of actually wearing one ...

Maeve was pulling out dresses and holding them up to me, while I stood there like a statue. Every dress she rejected was tossed to the floor.

'I think this one,' she said in the end, holding up a satin dress of pale, pale blue, with a long line of tiny pearly buttons all the way up the back. 'You put it on, and call me when you need help to button it up.'

I felt excited and sick as I pulled off my uniform, and put the dress over my head. The satin was soft and cool against my skin – I felt as if I were being hugged by an angel.

'Ready,' I said, and Maeve came in to button up the back of the dress.

'Now,' she said when she was finished. 'Let's see how you look.'

She twirled me around and we stood together

facing the long looking glass. It was a very strange moment. I looked like a fancy lady, and in her smock, Maeve could have been my servant.

Maeve saw it too. 'Look at us,' she laughed. 'We're all mixed up.'

* * *

Being painted is really quite nice. It was a treat to sit down on a lovely soft chair doing nothing in the middle of the day – usually I only sat down at meal times, and when I had sewing to do. It was very strange too, though. Downstairs, Nellie and the other servants were busy as always, and it didn't seem fair that Maeve had chosen me.

Maeve did a lot of sighing and walking up and down before she even picked up her paintbrush. But once she got started, she relaxed a bit, and we began to chat.

'Do you like being a housemaid?' she asked.

What kind of a question was that? It's not as if anyone asked my opinion. The job was arranged, and I did it. I still really wanted to be a teacher, but that seemed like an impossible dream now.

'Do you like being a fine lady?' I asked. Maeve laughed as if that were a very funny question, and then she repeated hers.

'Being a housemaid is all right,' I said. 'But sometimes I miss school.'

'I've never been to school.'

'But who taught you to read and write?'

'I have my governess, Miss Clayton. She can be a bit of a bore, but she's not too bad. We have lessons in the morning, and in the afternoon she teaches me how to be a lady. My mother was presented to Queen Victoria, you know.'

I didn't imagine I would ever be anywhere near a real live queen, but I wasn't jealous. Maeve's time with her governess didn't sound as much fun as the times I had with Rose and Hanora at school. For a

second, I felt sorry for this rich girl.

'Is it strange being the only pupil?' I asked.

'Oh, it's not just me – that would be unbearable. My very good friend Stella comes to lessons too. We tease Miss Clayton terribly. Sometimes she gets angry, but then Stella and I laugh at her.'

What would it be like to sit in Maeve's fine house and have lessons with her? What would it be like not to have to wear a uniform or spend your days cleaning someone else's home?

For a second I felt jealous of this girl Stella, who was allowed to be friends with Maeve.

'Stella is nice,' said Maeve. 'But she's two years younger than me – almost a child. I can't talk to her the way I talk to you.'

'Did you always live with Lady Georgina?' I asked quickly, trying not to let Maeve see how her last comment had pleased me.

'No. For some years I lived in Dublin with Mother and Father and my brother Stanislaus.'

'You've got a brother?'

'He's my half brother actually. He's at school in England now, so I hardly ever see him.'

My life seemed very boring compared to Maeve's. I'd love to go to Dublin, even for an hour, and here was Maeve casually mentioning that she'd lived there for years.

'And why did you come back to Sligo?'

'I think that's enough painting for today,' said Maeve, putting down her brush.

I knew I'd asked the wrong question, and ruined everything, but it was too late to change that now. Maybe Maeve would never speak to me again.

'We can continue tomorrow morning,' she said. 'I'll come and find you.'

'I'd like that,' I said, and she smiled a small smile that made me very happy.

'Can I see what you've done so far?' I asked.

'Absolutely not. Not even the tiniest peek until it's finished. But I can tell you I think it is turning out

very nicely.'

I was starting to feel excited. Maybe one day this portrait would hang in a big gallery in Dublin, and everyone would wonder who the young girl in the fine blue dress was.

'Look away, Lily,' said Maeve. 'While I put my easel safely in the corner.'

As I obediently looked away, I noticed some writing paper on the desk at the other side of the room. It was the most beautiful paper I had ever seen – pale cream with pink flowers all around the edges.

'Do you want some paper?' asked Maeve when she saw what I was looking at. 'You could write to your family if you wish.'

'No, thank you. My mam wouldn't like that – where I come from, letters mostly bring bad news.'

But then I thought of something. Nellie always snapped at me when I tried to ask her things or be nice to her. Maybe if I gave her a letter to read, she could see that I'm not her enemy.

'Could I write a short note to someone – one of my friends here – I want to thank her for something?'

'Of course,' said Maeve. 'Help yourself.'

I picked up the pen from the fancy silver penholder.

'Where is the inkwell?' I asked.

Maeve laughed. 'You don't need an inkwell. That's a fountain pen and the ink is already in it. Look, I'll show you.'

She came over and wasted a whole sheet of beautiful paper by drawing some swirly lines on it. It looked like magic to me. I could remember a long ago day at school when Hanora and I had a big fight over whose turn it was to fill up the inkwells. What would she say if she saw me with this fancy new pen that was already filled up with ink? Would there one day be a world where schools didn't have inkwells anymore?

Maeve handed me the pen. I didn't want her to see what I was writing, but I shouldn't have worried. She

went and sat on the bed looking at a book, almost as if I wasn't there.

I felt like a rich lady as I sat at the desk in my fine dress and picked up a sheet of writing paper. It was nothing like the floppy, almost see-through paper we used at school. I held it to my cheek, and got a faint scent of roses. I picked up the fountain pen and tried to work out what to say. In the end, this was the best I could do.

Dear Nellie. Thank you so much for saving my day off – that is one of the kindest things anyone has ever done for me. I know that sometimes you are cross with me, but that nice thing you did shows me that you really are a good person. I would like to be your friend. If you ever want to talk about anything, please come to me.

Your friend (I hope),

Lily

I carefully blotted what I had written, folded the note and went back into the dressing room. I took

off the fine dress, and put on my uniform, which now felt coarse against my skin. I slipped the note into the pocket of my apron.

Maeve came in as I was picking up all the dresses from the floor.

'Leave that,' she said. 'One of the maids can—'

Then she stopped herself. 'Let me help you,' she said.

I didn't like that idea at all, but before I could say anything she was busy tidying up. Last of all, she put the blue dress on a hanger.

'This is no use to me,' she said casually. 'It's much too small, and by the time Bridget is big enough, it will be hopelessly out of fashion. So you can have it if you like – why don't you take it away now?'

If I lived to a hundred, I would probably never again be offered so fine a present. But how could I accept?

How could I hang that perfect thing in the small cupboard that Nellie and I shared for our plain old

dresses?

Would people think I had stolen it?

Where could I wear such a thing without being laughed at for having pretensions?

So I took the dress and hung it back in the wardrobe. 'Thank you, Maeve,' I said. 'But, won't I need it for tomorrow's painting session? A different dress would look strange, wouldn't it?'

'As you wish,' said Maeve, and I suddenly felt that she didn't really care if I had the dress or not. She didn't know how much owning it would have meant to me. She had no idea what it was like to be me.

Just then the lunch bell rang.

'I've got to go,' I said, heading for the door.

'Thank you, Lily,' said Maeve. 'It's been fun.'

'I enjoyed it too,' I said. And then I left all the silk and lace behind and went back to my real life.

* * *

'It's late,' said Nellie, pulling her blanket over herself. 'Put on your nightgown and turn out the light so I can get some sleep. Not everyone is able to spend half the day sitting around with the gentry you know. Some of us have done a whole day's work.'

I took the letter from the pocket of my apron, and held it towards her. I'd been putting off the moment, not knowing how she would react.

'This is for you,' I said.

Nellie looked at the page suspiciously. 'What is it?'

'I wrote you a letter,' I said. The letter had seemed like a good idea when I was in Maeve's bedroom, but now I felt a bit stupid. Who writes a letter to some-one they spend most of the day with?

Nellie kept her hands under the blankets, almost as if the letter might bite her.

'I don't want your letter,' she said.

I could feel tears coming to my eyes. How could I get through to this sad, angry girl?

'But I wrote it specially for you,' I said, holding it

closer. 'And it smells nice.'

Slowly, Nellie brought one hand out from under the blanket. She took the letter, held it to her nose and breathed deeply. She unfolded the letter, and then quickly folded it back together again, and slipped it under her pillow.

At least she had taken it, but I still wasn't happy.

'You didn't even read it,' I said.

'Who do you think I am?' she snapped. 'Some fancy lady who gets letters for nothing? Well, I'm not. I'm a servant and so are you – though you seem to forget that most of the time. I don't have time for reading letters, and if you were doing your job properly you wouldn't have time for writing them either.'

And then she took the letter from under her pillow, crumpled it up, and threw it across the room.

Chapter Twelve

ext morning, Nellie didn't even speak to me. I tried to say a few things to her, but she always turned away, as if my voice was hurting her ears. After a while I began to wish she was shouting at me, because the silence was so strange and awkward.

After lunch, Nellie and I settled down to our sewing. We were mending sheets, which is a very boring job, so my mind was wandering. I kept thinking about Maeve – I hadn't seen her that day, and I wondered if she had forgotten about painting my portrait. Had she already moved on to something else more exciting than me?

Just when it looked as if I was reaching the end of my sewing bundle, Mrs Bailey came in with a fine green silk dress, and handed it to me.

'Lady Mary has noticed how neat your stitches are,

Lily,' she said. 'And she especially asked for you to fix this rip on the sleeve of her favourite gown.'

I'm proud of my good work, but I felt a bad taste in my mouth. Next to me, Nellie was viciously stabbing a sheet with her needle, almost as if she wanted to kill it. For a second I wished my stitching was poor, so she wouldn't have one more reason to hate me.

I sewed the sleeve carefully, and when I was finished, the tear was invisible. Reluctantly I folded the smooth silk, and returned to patching the last of the boring linen sheets. I began to daydream – if I couldn't become a teacher, maybe one day I could get a job as a seamstress, making fine gowns for rich ladies like Lady Mary. Maybe one day I could have my own shop, where ...

Just then, Maeve rushed into the room.

'Sorry, Lily,' she said. 'I had a very busy morning. First, Albert was showing me how to fix the motor car, and after that Uncle Joss wanted me to help him in the greenhouse. He's breeding some new daffodils

and he's very excited about them.'

I looked at her in surprise. I couldn't imagine a fine lady dirtying her hands with engines or gardens. But then, I was beginning to see that Maeve wasn't like most fine ladies.

'Anyway, better late than never, come on and let's get started.'

Maeve ran from the room, and after a sigh and a nod from Mrs Bailey, I followed her.

* * *

This time it felt a little less strange to be sitting in Maeve's room, all dressed up in the blue silk. Once again, Maeve took a while to get started. She wandered around the room, picking things up and putting them down again. She showed me a bundle of fabrics, in all colours of the rainbow.

'My Aunt Mabel sent me a present all the way from England,' she said. 'There's enough for five

new dresses.'

I didn't know what to say to this. I had barely owned five dresses in my whole life – and most of those had belonged to someone else before me. Once, one of Mam's cousins in America sent us a few yards of navy blue fabric. Next to Maeve's silk and satin, I fear it would have looked very rough and cheap, but at the time, I thought it was the finest fabric ever made. Mam set to work quickly. Winnie and Anne needed new dresses, and the boys needed shirts for school. By the time all of those were made, there was only enough left for a scarf for me, and a hanky for Mam.

'What do you think?' asked Maeve, tossing the fabrics towards the bed, where they floated down softly, like dandelion seeds in a breeze.

'I think you're very lucky,' I said. 'It must be lovely to have all that fabric just for you. It must be lovely not to have to share anything.'

'Don't be jealous,' she said. 'I have to share my mother with all of Ireland.'

'What do you mean?'

'Mother wants to do everything and fix everything.'

'Like what?'

'She's in all kinds of organisations – daughters of Ireland, Fianna Eireann – and probably more that we don't even know about. No one in the family talks about her very much, except for Aunt Eva, and that's not any good to me, because she's hardly ever here either.'

'It sounds as if your mother has a very exciting life,' I said.

'It's exciting but she works hard too. She fights for votes for women, and extra food for the poor. She is an exceedingly brave person.'

'You must be very proud of her,' I said, thinking of my own poor mam who was brave too, but never had time for anything except feeding and caring for her children.

'I *am* proud,' said Maeve. 'Since the Lockout started she's been helping starving children, you know, and

that's a very good thing, but ...'

'What?'

'I wouldn't change Mother, or what she believes in, and I know she thinks it's best for me to be here with Gaga, as she is so busy in Dublin.'

So that's why Maeve had to live with her granny – her mother and father were too busy to take care of her. Poor Maeve. I could see how much she missed her mam and dad. I could also see she wasn't used to talking about this. I wanted to put my arms around her, but I didn't dare to move.

'I would like to see Mother and Father more often,' she said. 'Uncle Joss and Aunt Mary see their little ones at least once a day, when the nurses bring them down for their goodnight kisses. Sometimes Aunt Mary takes Michael and Hugh for riding lessons and spends the whole afternoon watching them from the gallery.'

I had to smile. My mam saw Winnie and Anne almost every second of every day. Winnie spent most

of her days clinging to her skirts, and Anne was never more than a shout away.

'It must be nice when your mother visits you here,' I said, trying to cheer her up.

'It is,' said Maeve. 'I love seeing her. Mother respects me and talks to me as if I were a grown-up.'

'That's nice,' I said. Now I felt even more sorry for her. I like being treated as a grown-up by everyone else, but I'll always be my mam's little girl – that's the way things are supposed to be.

'You'll see Mother soon enough,' said Maeve. 'She will be visiting at Christmas – and maybe my father too – though he might have to go to Poland to see his family.'

'The Countess will be here at Christmas?'

I had heard so much about her, it was almost as if she wasn't a real person at all. Soon, though, she would really be here, under the same roof as me! I could hardly believe what Maeve was saying, and I was already in a panic.

'What should I say to her if I meet her? What should I do? Should I bow or curtsey? What should I call her – Your Highness or Countess or Your Majesty, or what?'

Maeve laughed. 'She's just a woman – and she won't care what you call her as long as you are nice to her dog. If you do say something to her she probably won't even notice – she is always busy and she'll be running around like a whirlwind. Anyway, enough about Mother. We've got work to do.'

For a long time, she concentrated on her painting, and I sat there watching her. I was older than Maeve, but she was much more sophisticated and well-travelled than me – she had been all over Ireland, to places I'd only heard about. In some ways though, Maeve seemed very young. She'd never made a bed, or scrubbed a floor, or done anything to earn a living. She wasn't even allowed outside the grounds on her own. She was always protected and minded and watched over. It seemed like a very strange life

to me.

Finally, Maeve put down her brush with a big sigh. 'This portrait really isn't turning out so well,' she said.

'Can I….?'

'No! You can't see. I'm not proud of this one at all.'

As she said the words, she grabbed the page and tore it into tiny pieces.

'I'm sorry,' I said. 'I…'

'Oh, don't worry,' she said with a big smile. 'It's not your fault. We've got lots of time. We can start all over again tomorrow.'

I couldn't smile with her. Sitting in this fancy room was very nice, but how long before the other servants punished me for doing something I had no choice about at all?

* * *

I was still worried when I went into the servants dining hall for supper. I went towards my usual place,

but stopped when I noticed that everyone was staring at me. I checked that my cap was on straight, and that I didn't have any terrible stains on my apron, but I couldn't find anything wrong.

'Look at Miss Fancy,' said one man, and everyone laughed.

'Pretty as a picture,' said another, which made everyone laugh even more.

'Get out your paintbrushes, lads,' said another. 'The model is here.'

The teasing went on and on. Nearly everyone had something clever to say. I put my head down and walked towards my place with tears in my eyes. This was so unfair.

And then Maggie, the laundry maid, stepped towards the laughing men, shaking her fist.

'Leave her alone, the whole lot of you. None of this is Lily's fault. She's only doing what she's told – like we all have to do. So you can shut your faces.'

'Or what?' asked one lad, pretending to look scared.

'I'm shaking in my boots.'

'Or I'll.....' Maggie was tiny, and even though she had a fierce look in her eyes, I had no idea what she was supposed to do now. It was nice of her to stand up for me, but I didn't want her to suffer for it.

'What's all this noise about? What's going on?'

It was Mr Kilgallon, and he did not look happy.

'Nothing, sir,' said one of the men.

'Just a joke,' said another.

Now Mrs Bailey came in. She looked at the men, and then she saw me with my big red face, and the stupid tears, which were now dripping down my cheeks and onto my apron. She knew everything that happened amongst the servants and I'm sure it didn't take her long to work out what the 'joke' was.

'If there's any more of this, there'll be no cakes for a week,' she said. 'Do you all understand?'

Now the men looked like little children whose toys had been taken away from them.

The man who had started it all looked at me, and

seemed surprised to see my tears. 'I'm truly sorry,' he said. 'We didn't mean any harm – and I'll make sure it doesn't happen again.'

I could see he meant what he said. I'd noticed that he was a man that the others all listened to, so I nodded to show him that it was all right.

'Thank you, for standing up for me, Maggie,' I whispered as we sat down. 'That was brave of you.'

'Anything for a friend,' said Maggie, and then we all had our supper.

Chapter Thirteen

That night I got to our room before Nellie did. I picked up the crumpled letter that was still in the corner of the room – (we didn't have any servants to clean up after us!) I smoothed it out and read it again. It was a nice letter, and I was sure that if only Nellie would read it, she'd understand what I was trying to say to her.

When she came in a few minutes later, she saw the letter in my hand, and took a step away, almost as if this small sheet of paper frightened her.

'Just read it, please,' I said. 'And then I'll stop talking about it, I promise.'

But she didn't take the letter from me. Instead she sat on her bed and started to cry. This was so unexpected, I didn't have any idea what to do. Nellie always seemed so strong and so tough. What had I

done to make her cry like this?

I went and sat beside her, and patted her shoulder. I couldn't tell if she liked that, but she didn't pull away. I leaned over to put the letter on her locker, and all of a sudden the truth came to me, and I wondered how I hadn't seen it before.

'Oh, Nellie,' I whispered. 'Can you read at all?'

She looked up at me for a second, and then she began to cry even more. She hadn't answered my question, but I knew I was right. I kept on patting her shoulder, and saying 'Shhh now, don't cry,' the way I did with Winnie when she was upset.

And then Nellie was angry. 'Everything is so easy for you,' she said pushing me away. 'With your own mam and your own home, and your lovely school and all your friends. Do you think I had any of that in the workhou—?'

She stopped herself, but she knew it was too late. I wanted to tell her that it wasn't a surprise to me, that Isabelle had told me about all that ages ago, but

I didn't know if that would make things even worse.

'I'm so sorry you were in the workhouse, Nellie,' I said. 'It must have been terrible, but it's not your fault. You don't have to be ashamed.'

'Easy for you to say,' she sniffed.

My childhood hadn't been perfect, but compared to Nellie, I'd had a wonderful life. 'I'm sorry you didn't have what I had,' I said. 'I'm sorry if there was no school in the workhouse.'

Now she stared at me with her huge blue eyes.

'There was a school,' she whispered. 'But ... but there were so many children ... more than a hundred sometimes ... and the Mistress was very cross ... she had a big stick ... and mostly I was too sick to go to school. When I was well, I couldn't catch up ... I didn't understand ... and she beat me ... and ...'

Remembering it all made her cry some more. This time I put my arms around her and held her tight.

'Now you know the truth you will hate me,' she said, when she pulled away from me. 'Just like every-

one else. No one ever wants to be friends with a workhouse girl.'

I wanted to cry. It was true that Nellie had no friends in Lissadell, but that wasn't because she'd once been in a workhouse. It was because she scared everyone away with her bad temper and grumpy comments – but because she was so snappy, I couldn't even tell her that.

'I don't hate you, Nellie,' I said. 'I want to be your friend. Listen to what I wrote and maybe you'll understand.'

I picked up the letter and read it aloud. For a long time Nellie didn't say anything.

'Don't you like it?' I asked.

'I like it,' she said. 'I like it very much – and I'm sorry for crumpling it up after you went to so much trouble ... but I don't deserve it.'

I was disappointed, but then I realised that was stupid of me. Poor Nellie had been sad for so long, I couldn't expect her to be immediately happy, just because I gave her a letter and said a few nice things

to her.

Still, I was glad when she took the letter from me and put it under her pillow again. Then she stood up and took off her apron.

'Time to get ready for bed,' she said. I knew she wanted to end the conversation, but for all I knew, Nellie would never talk like this to me again, and there was one more thing I had to know.

'Your family,' I said. 'Are they ... ?'

'My mam and dad had the fever, and they died. That's why my sisters and me had to go to the work-house.'

'I'm so sorry to hear that,' I said. 'But your sisters ... ?

'They split us up when we got to the workhouse – they always do. And I was only little and it was a long time ago, so ... if my sisters fetched up here, I might not even recognise them any more. Sometimes I dream about them, but I never see their faces prop-erly – all I can see is their long red hair, just like mine.'

I thought about my sisters and brothers. Seeing

them once a week never seemed enough. What would I do if I didn't see them for years and years? What would I do if it was so long, I couldn't recognise those sweet faces any more?

'I'm sorry, Nellie.' It was all I could think of to say. 'I'm so, so sorry.'

When my brothers and sisters were sad, I was usually able to help them. I rubbed Winnie's tummy when it was sore, and I hugged Anne when she fell and scraped her knees. If the boys were fighting with their friends, I could usually sort things out.

But how could I help Nellie? I couldn't make her parents come back to life. I couldn't march into the workhouse, and demand to see her sisters, and bring them back to Lissadell with me. I was only a poor housemaid, and there was nothing I could do.

During the night I woke to hear Nellie crying. I leaned out of bed, found her hand and held it tight. When morning came my fingers were stiff and sore, but I didn't mind.

Chapter Fourteen

*A*fter breakfast, Mrs Bailey gave me the nice easy job of tidying Lady Mary's dressing table. Lady Mary had so many pots of creams and powders – no wonder she had such soft, perfect skin. My poor mam's face was always red and sore looking, and she never owned as much as one pot of cream to make it better. Maybe I could buy her some when I got my wages.

Just as I was straightening up Lady Mary's silver hairbrush and comb, Maeve came and found me. She looked beautiful with a fur-trimmed cloak over her elegant green striped dress.

'No painting today, I'm afraid, Lily,' she said.

'Oh,' I said, trying not to sound too disappointed. I had been looking forward to sitting in Maeve's lovely bedroom and chatting – and scrubbing the dining

room floor wasn't going to be much of a consolation.

'I don't know when we will be able to paint again. Gaga and I are going to stay with some of her ancient old cousins in Galway. We'll be gone for ages and ages, and it's going to be so boring.'

I tried not to smile. I wouldn't mind being a visitor in some fine house. As far as I could see, being bored had to be better than working all day long.

'We'll do more painting when I get back, all right?'

I nodded. Maeve was the one actually doing the painting, while all I had to do was sit still and look like myself, but I realised that the whole thing meant more to me than it did to her. She had a busy life of travel and hobbies, schoolwork and parties, and my life was ... well it was nothing like that.

* * *

Next day, Lady Mary came in while I was sweeping the drawing room. I moved to the side and looked

down at a rug, as if it were the most beautiful rug ever made.

'Ah, Lily,' she said. 'As you know, Christmas is coming.'

Of course I knew Christmas was coming, but I wasn't looking forward to it like I used to. At home, Mam always found time to knit a present for each of us. It was usually something useful like new socks, or a warm vest, but she could make it special by adding in some brightly coloured wool or even a scrap of ribbon. No matter how bad things were, Mam always managed to get a chicken for our dinner on Christmas day, and after we'd eaten, we'd go to a neighbour's house and sing songs and tell stories till well after our usual bedtimes.

Already Maggie had told me about Christmas in Lissadell, and it didn't sound like much fun for the servants. There were many visitors, some of whom stayed for a week or longer – and more visitors meant more work for us.

Lady Mary hadn't asked a question, but she seemed to be waiting for me to say something.

'Yes, Lady Mary,' I said, with my eyes still fixed on the rug. 'Christmas will be nice.'

'This year I plan to buy a little something for all of the servants, so I was wondering what you would like?'

Was I hearing right?

Was she offering to buy me a present?

'I ... I ...'

'Don't be so shy. I'm sure there is something you would like, so tell me what it is and I will do my best to get it for you.'

Now I could hardly breathe. There were so many things I would like, but how could I pick one?

If I chose something too big, would Lady Mary think me impossibly greedy and end up buying me nothing at all?

If I chose something small, would I feel cheated when I saw the presents the other servants asked

for? Mam always says I shouldn't compare myself to other people, but how would I feel if everyone else got something better than me?

And then the words popped out. 'I'd ... if it's not too much to ask ... I'd very much like a doll.'

'A doll?'

Lady Mary didn't sound cross, so I continued. 'Yes, if you wouldn't mind, I would love a doll of my own. I've never had one before, and if I got one, I would love it, and on my days off I could bring it home and let my little sisters play with it, but I would tell them to be very careful, and ...'

'Of course you shall have a doll. Is there any particular type of doll you would like?'

I remembered the beautiful doll I had seen in the nursery. 'I'd be happy with any kind at all,' I said. 'But if I could get a doll with curly hair, and a satin dress with lace on it, I think I might be the happiest girl in all of Sligo.'

Lady Mary laughed. 'I think that could be arranged,'

she said. Then she took a tiny notebook and pencil from her pocket, and I watched as she wrote *Lily*, and next to it the beautiful words – *doll, curly hair, satin dress.*

I felt like jumping up and down for joy, but was afraid that might spoil everything, so I had to be content with a little skip, as I got back to my sweeping.

Chapter Fifteen

On workdays I found it very hard to climb out of my warm bed, but on Saturdays this was never a problem.

Nellie was still sitting on her bed rubbing her eyes, while I was already dressed and ready to go. As always, I was excited, but I had to bottle up my feelings. How could I let Nellie see how happy I was when she had no trips home to look forward to?

How could I talk about my mam, when she had no mam at all?

'I'll see you tonight, then,' I said.

'Yes,' said Nellie. 'And I hope you have a lovely time with your mam and your brothers and sisters.'

'Thank you. It's nice of you to say that, since ... well ...'

She shrugged. 'You're my friend. I want you to be

happy.'

'Saying that I'm your friend makes me very happy,' I said. 'And I wish you could be happy too.'

'Thank you,' she whispered. I smiled at her, but I think we both wondered how my wish could possibly come true.

It was too early for breakfast, but I knew cook would find me something to eat. She was being extra-nice to me since I'd mended her best dress a few days earlier.

'Ah, my favourite little seamstress,' she said when she saw me. 'Sit yourself down and I'll have the scullery maid bring you some bread and hot milk and maybe a nice egg to keep you going on your journey.'

Cook laughed when I cleaned my plate, and had second helpings too. 'Slow down, Lily,' she said. 'You're eating as if you weren't going to see food again for a month.'

My mouth was too full to answer her, but I didn't know what to say anyway. How could I explain that

I didn't like to eat much at home? Every scrap I ate was one less for everyone else, and it hurt me to see Winnie's skinny little legs, and Mam's fake smile when she said she had enough, even when she'd barely had a thing.

But maybe cook understood anyway. She went into the pantry and a few minutes later she came back with a basket covered with a clean white cloth.

'I ordered a bit too much this week,' she said, as she handed the basket to me. 'And I wouldn't like to see it spoil. It would be a great help to me if you could give these few small things to your mam.'

I pulled back the cloth to see a basket full of treasure. There were eggs and carrots and parsnips and cheese and a big hunk of fruit cake.

'Oh, Cook,' I said. 'My mam will—'

'I forgot something,' she said, and she ran back into the pantry, coming back with something large wrapped in brown paper. 'A little bit of ham,' she said as she put it into the basket, and tucked the cloth

neatly around everything.

Meat of any kind was a big treat in our house, and this looked like the biggest piece of ham we'd ever had.

'Thank you so much,' I said. 'You are truly kind and my mam will remember this day forever.'

Cook looked embarrassed. 'Get along with you,' she said. 'Or it'll be time for you to come back before you even get to the gate.'

* * *

Mam met me in the front yard and she cried when she saw what was in the basket. That made Winnie cry too, and then Anne, who never liked to be left out of anything, joined in too.

'No, don't cry, sillies,' I said. 'Mam is happy.'

They looked puzzled at first, but when she saw that Mam was smiling through her tears, Anne started to dance around in circles. Winnie copied her, and

then Mam and I joined in. The four of us held hands and danced around the yard like wild things, and we didn't care if anyone saw us. In the end, Mam threw herself down on the bench and the girls jumped on top of her. I sat beside them as we all laughed and tried to catch our breath.

'Oh, Lily,' said Mam putting her arm around me. 'That laugh makes me feel ten years younger.'

I lay my head on her shoulder and enjoyed the moment. It was so nice not having to worry if my hair was messy, or if I was being polite enough, or quiet enough, or obedient enough. That's what I missed about home. I missed being me.

* * *

Later, while I was helping Mam to put the food in the cool cupboard in the back yard, I told her all about Nellie.

'The poor little pet,' she said. 'What a life she's had.

Still though, now she's had a piece of luck.'

'What do you mean?'

'She got the best girl in all of Ireland as a friend, and that's a rare treat.'

'Thank you, Mam.'

'I love hearing all your stories from the Big House,' she said. 'Thinking about my Lily serving all them fancy people gives me a lift. I'm sad when you're not here, but I look forward to you telling me every little thing about your new life.'

Now I felt guilty. I hadn't told Mam about Maeve and the painting, and I didn't intend to. It was the first big secret there had ever been between us, and it had been making me feel uncomfortable all morning. When I'm trying hard not to say something, I'm always afraid that the words are going to jump out all on their own.

But how could I tell Mam the truth?

I'd heard Lady Mary and Sir Josslyn talking, and I'd seen little signs that the world is changing. In

the servants' hall there was talk of all kinds of new things like votes for women, and freedom for Ireland. Mam wasn't like me though. She was still living in the olden days. She was happy for me to be spending time with Nellie, but she would never understand the friendship that was growing between Maeve and me. If she knew the truth, she'd be cross with me. She'd say I was getting above myself. Worst of all, she'd worry for me, and she already had plenty to worry about.

Then I remembered my good news.

'Lady Mary is so kind,' I said. 'She's buying presents for all the servants.'

'A present from the gentry,' said Mam. 'Aren't you the lucky girl? I wonder what she'll get you?'

'Oh, she asked me what I wanted, so I know already what it's going to be.'

'And what's that?'

'It's going to be a beautiful doll, all of my own. I'm going to call her Julianne. I can make clothes for her

and she'll be gorgeous. She'll have long dark hair and—'

'A doll? You asked Lady Mary for a doll?' Mam didn't look very happy.

'Yes. Do you think that was too much? But Lady Mary didn't seem to mind – and I want a doll so badly, and I can bring her home every week so Winnie and Anne can play with her too. They can dress her up and ...'

'You'll have to tell Lady Mary you'd like a pair of winter boots.'

'But I've already said—'

'You'll have to tell her you've changed your mind. This is a great opportunity, Lily, and you can't waste it on dolls. Lady Mary can buy the best quality boots, so they will last you for years, and then Anne and Winnie can have them after you.'

I could feel tears coming to my eyes, but how could I let Mam see them, when I knew she was right? My only boots were much too small for me, so it made

sense to ask for a new pair. Dolls were for rich people who didn't have to worry about what to wear on their feet.

Mam put her arm around me, and I saw there were tears in her eyes too. It wasn't her fault we were poor.

'I know you'd like a doll, Lily,' she said. 'But ...'

'It's all right, Mam,' I said, pretending I was wiping a speck of dust out of my eyes. 'I don't know what I was thinking. I'll tell Lady Mary I've changed my mind.'

* * *

The rest of the day went quickly. I cleaned the windows and helped Mam to wash the bedsheets.

'This isn't much of a day off for you, Lily,' she said. In a way she was right, but the girls were small and the boys were at school all week. If I didn't help Mam, then she had to do everything herself, and that didn't seem fair.

'It doesn't matter,' I said. 'I like helping you.'

When the jobs were done, I went for a walk with Hanora and Rose, and after that, I helped the boys with their homework. When we were finished, Anne came over to the table with a battered old copy book and a little scrap of pencil.

'Time for my homework,' she said.

I smiled and I leaned over to take the copy from her, but she went past me and handed it to Denis.

'I've been helping Anne with her letters,' he said, looking a bit embarrassed. 'She'll be starting school soon, and I want her to do well.'

'She knows lots already,' said Jimmy.

'You clever girl!' I said. 'You'll be top of the class when you get to school, and we'll be the proudest family in Sligo.'

I *was* happy that Denis was teaching Anne, and that she was doing so well, but I couldn't help feeling jealous. I used to be the one who helped the girls with everything, and it hurt a little bit to see that

Denis could do just as well as me.

He looked really proud as he held Anne's small hand in his, and helped to guide the pencil along the page.

And then I thought of Nellie – I'd been so busy thinking of all the ways I couldn't help her, I'd never taken time to consider the one thing I could do. I could teach her to read!

I was so excited, I leaned over and gave Denis a huge kiss on the cheek.

'Yuck!' he said, wiping his face with the side of his hand. 'What was that for?'

'Because you've given me a wonderful idea.'

'Well, we're trying to work here, so don't do it again,' he said, and we all laughed.

Chapter Sixteen

*a*s soon as I got back to Lissadell, I went straight up to the nursery. Isabelle was in the dressing room, folding the children's clothes. Each of the little Gore-Booth children had more clothes than my entire family.

'I'll be finished in a minute, Lily,' she said. 'Why don't you go in and look at that doll you love so much?'

I went and picked up the doll and rocked her in my arms. Now I knew I'd never have a doll of my own, playing with this one made me sad, so I stroked her hair, and fixed her dress, and put her back on the chair.

'Tell me all about your trip home.' said Isabelle. 'Did you have a lovely time with your family?'

'It was wonderful, thank you,' I said. 'I want to talk

to you about something else though.'

I looked over my shoulder to see if the nurse was around. She was always kind to the children, but I was a bit afraid of her in her starchy white uniform and shiny black shoes.

'Don't worry,' said Isabelle. 'Nurse is downstairs having a natter in Mrs Bailey's sitting room, and the children are fast asleep. It's just us here.'

'It's about Nellie,' I began.

I told Isabelle all about the letter I'd written, and how Nellie hadn't been able to read it.

'But don't tell anyone else,' I said. 'I don't think that would be fair to Nellie.'

'Of course, I won't say a word.'

I smiled at her. I knew she wasn't a gossip, like some of the kitchen maids.

'Anyway, I'm only telling you because I have a plan. I'm going to teach Nellie to read, and I need you to lend me some of the children's books – I'll take good care of them, I promise.'

'That's such a lovely thing to do,' said Isabelle. 'And I'm sure I'll be able to get some books – the children have more than they could read in a lifetime. I'll check with Nurse when she comes back, and I'll bring some books to your room later.'

* * *

When I got to my room after supper, there was a neat stack of books on my bed. Some were very easy, with A B Cs and numbers. Some had pictures with words underneath, and some were stories of magical places. There was also a tiny chalkboard and a box of coloured chalks.

I changed into my nightgown, folded my clothes and put them away. Nellie was still working, so I wrapped Mam's shawl around my shoulders and jumped into bed. I picked up one of the story books, and began to turn the pages. I'd never before had the luxury of a whole room to myself, a gas light and

something exciting to read – it felt like being in heaven.

Much later Nellie came into the room yawning.

'I am so tired,' she said. 'Mrs Bailey had me take out all the living room rugs and beat them, and I think my poor back is broken.'

'I'm sorry,' I said, putting down my book. 'I'll do them with you next time.'

'Thank you. Did you have a nice day with your mam?'

'Yes – and while I was there I had a wonderful idea. I thought ...'

Now I felt shy.

Would Nellie feel insulted if I tried to help her?

Would she think I was treating her like a baby?

Would she be angry with me?

Now that we were starting to be friends, I didn't want to do anything that might spoil it.

But friends look out for each other, so I had to try.

'Maybe I could teach you how to read?'

At first Nellie didn't say anything, and I started to worry. When she did speak, her voice was so low, I could hardly hear her.

'You'd do that for me?'

I jumped out of bed and hugged her.

'Of course I'd do that for you. When do you want to start?'

'Now?'

So she changed into her nightgown, and snuggled into my bed with me, and her lessons began.

* * *

For the next few days there was no sign of Maeve. Sometimes I went into her room to dust and air it. Sometimes it felt as if I had imagined my days with her. Had I really worn her fine dress, and sat on her soft chair? Had she really talked about her life and asked about mine? If it weren't for the easel and paints in the corner of the room, I might almost have

imagined the whole thing.

* * *

And then one morning she was back!

She found me coming out of Lady Mary's room.

'There you are, Lily,' she said. 'I've been looking everywhere for you.'

'Lissadell is a big place,' I said. 'In my mam's house, if you're not in the kitchen then you're in the bedroom – it's hard to get lost.'

Maeve laughed, and I realised how much it meant to me that I could make her do this.

'Hurry up,' she said. 'We've lost so many days, and I want to get started on the new work straight away. I've already cleared it with Mrs B, so you can just come along with me.'

In her room, she'd set up the easel with a clean sheet of paper, and the soft chair was all ready for me by the window.

Maeve went into the dressing room, and took out the blue dress, but suddenly I felt daring. She had so many beautiful dresses, and I thought how nice it would be to try another one.

'Maybe the blue wasn't right after all,' I said. 'Maybe I could ...?'

Maeve laughed. 'I *love* playing dress up. Wait there a minute – I know where there's lots of old clothes belonging to Mother and my aunts.'

She ran from the room, and a minute later she was back with an armful of dresses and a huge box of hats and gloves and jewellery and shoes.

'You first,' she said. 'Which dress would you like?'

When I was dressed in a gorgeous purple silk dress, with lace at the neck, Maeve gave me a feathered hat, and fur-trimmed gloves and a long string of pearls.

'What do you think?' she said, as I tried to balance in the silver high-heeled shoes I'd chosen. I couldn't speak. A stranger was staring back at me from the mirror.

'Come on,' she said. 'Let's try something else.'

For a long time the two of us tried on dresses and jewellery and hats and shoes. We stood in front of the mirror and made faces, and walked up and down like fine ladies – (we looked alike, except Maeve was practising and I was dreaming.)

In the end, Maeve threw herself onto her bed, and I sat on my usual chair by the window.

'That hat you've got on belongs to my mother,' said Maeve. 'But I think it's nicer on you.'

She was giving me a compliment, but I didn't care. All I could think of was that I was wearing Countess Markievicz's hat! Maybe wearing her clothes was making me feel brave, so I brought up something that had been on my mind for a long time.

'Why won't anyone around here talk about your mother?' I asked.

Maeve sighed. 'Everyone except Aunt Eva thinks Mother should spend her time going to parties and balls – acting like a lady. Instead she does all kinds of

things that people here think make her a disgrace to the family.'

'And what do you think?'

'I'm proud of the way Mother stands up for poor people, and I am happy that she is working for a free Ireland, but sometimes she can be rather ... dramatic.'

'She's an actress?'

'That's not what I meant – though she does appear on the stage sometimes – even in the Abbey Theatre.'

'I've never heard of that before. Is it in Sligo?

Maeve laughed, but not in a mean way. 'No. It's a very famous theatre in Dublin.'

'I must have missed it on my last visit to the capital,' I said. 'I might have had too much shopping to do.'

Now the two of us laughed. We both knew I'd only been to Sligo once, and had never been anywhere near Dublin.

'So when your mother isn't on stage, what does she do that's so dramatic?' I asked.

'Well, once she was arrested.'

'For what?' I hoped Maeve wasn't insulted by the shock in my voice. In my village, people only got arrested for stealing or fighting, but surely Maeve's mother wouldn't do anything like that?

'She was at a demonstration, and she said some bad things and threw gravel at a policeman – it was reported in the *Sligo Champion*. Mother wrote to Uncle Joss and told him that the story wasn't true, but I don't think he believed her. He wasn't happy, I can tell you.'

'I can believe that,' I said, thinking of Sir Josslyn who seemed so calm and sensible and proper.

'Mother was always a bit wild,' said Maeve. 'Even when she was young. Once she and Aunt Eva stole a cow and her calf.'

'What did they do that for – they surely didn't need the milk?'

'They did it just for fun. They hid the animals, and spied on the poor farmer who spent the whole night

searching the lanes, calling "sucky, sucky".'

At the thought of it, we both had a fit of laughing, which kept going until there was a loud knock on the door.

'Miss Maeve. Is everything all right?'

It was a man's voice.

'Miss Maeve?'

It was Mr Kilgallon!

I jumped up, almost tripping on my long velvet dress. The room was a mess, with clothes and jewellery thrown all over the floor and on the bed.

Maeve was perfectly relaxed. 'It's all right,' she said quietly. 'I asked you here, so you won't be in trouble – and anyway, Kilgallon and I are good friends. When I was little and had no companions, he used to play football with me on the landing. Don't panic.'

But it was too late for that. My hands were shaking as I tried to gather up bundles of clothes.

'Miss Maeve, may I come in?'

I didn't wait for her to answer. I dropped the bundle

of dresses and ran into the dressing room, where I
hid behind a tall screen.

'Yes, you may come in,' said Maeve, and I heard the
door opening.

For a minute there was no other sound, then Mr
Kilgallon spoke again.

'I heard some strange noises. Is everything all right?'
He sounded more worried than angry, but that might
change if he saw me all dressed up like a lady.

'Everything's perfectly fine, thank you,' said Maeve.
'I've been playing dressing up. My friend Stella is in
London, and until my cousins come from England, I
have no one my own age to play with.'

'You poor little girl.' I had to peep from behind
the screen to make sure that it was still Mr Kilgallon.
His voice sounded all soft and soppy, nothing like the
way he usually spoke to the servants.

'The days are very long and I get so lonely all on
my own,' said Maeve.

I smiled. Maeve's mother might have been an

actress, but I couldn't imagine that she was better than this girl.

'Your room is rather untidy,' said Mr Kilgallon. 'I'll send one of the maids up.'

Now I had to cover my mouth to hide a sudden fit of giggling. What would he say if he knew that one of the maids was already there, all dressed up in velvet and lace?

'No, thank you,' said Maeve. 'No need. I'll have it tidy in no time – it will give me something to do.'

'If you're sure?'

'I'm very sure. Thank you. Goodbye.'

I heard the door closing, and I waited a minute before tiptoeing into the bedroom.

'All's clear,' said Maeve. 'Now give me a hand with this or I'll be here all night.'

Chapter Seventeen

That night Nellie and I stayed up late, practising her reading. She was doing very well, and could already read quite a few words. I was tired, though. My eyes kept closing and once or twice I actually fell asleep, but I couldn't say anything. Nellie was so enthusiastic, and I didn't want to spoil it for her.

In the morning I was exhausted. 'I don't know what's got into you, girl,' said Mrs Bailey, the second time she had to correct me for missing patches when I was polishing the big dining table. 'You are normally so reliable, but this morning, I don't know where your head is.'

I knew where my head was. It was all mixed up with memories of my fun morning with Maeve, and my late night of teaching Nellie.

In the afternoon, there was a big pile of mending

to be done, so Nellie and I settled down with our sewing baskets. I had always liked sewing, and now that Nellie and I were friends, it was even nicer. We were chatting happily when Lady Mary came in.

'Lily,' she said. 'I wonder if I could have a word?'

'Yes, Lady Mary,' I said, resting my sewing on my knee, and waiting for her to continue.

'Not here,' she said. 'Please follow me.'

As I stood up, I could feel my knees shaking. She must have heard about me wearing Countess Markievicz's clothes. Was she taking me outside so she could fire me? If she let me go without a letter of recommendation, I'd never find another position. My family would go hungry without the extra money I was bringing in. Denis and Jimmy would have to leave school. The little ones ...

I looked at Nellie. She gave me a small smile, but I could see she was worried too.

I followed Lady Mary along the corridor and up the big staircase. It felt like the longest walk of my

life. Why couldn't she just fire me and get it over with? Was this walk part of my punishment? We went along an upstairs corridor, and into the small room she used for writing letters. She walked to the window, and I couldn't take it any more.

'I'm so sorry, Lady Mary,' I said. 'I'm truly very sorry, and it won't happen again.'

She turned towards me and smiled. 'What are you sorry for?'

I put my head down. Was she teasing me?

'Lily, have you done something wrong?'

I'd only done what Maeve had told me to do, and maybe that was wrong, but if Lady Mary didn't know about it ...

'I don't think so – but since you brought me here I was afraid you were cross with me.'

'Not at all,' she said, turning back to the window. 'I brought you here because one of these curtains is damaged, and as you are the best needleworker in the house, I thought perhaps you could mend it for me?'

I was so relieved I felt like jumping up and down on the table, but that might not have turned out well, so I put my head down. 'Of course, Lady Mary,' I said. 'I'll get my things and start at once.'

'Oh, and there's something else I wanted to mention to you. Did you know that Lady Georgina set up a needlework school some years ago? It was for the women on the estate, so they could learn a skill, and earn some extra money.'

'No, Lady Mary, I didn't know that. It was nice of her.'

She continued. 'Maybe one day you'd like to—'

'Show some of my needlework to the ladies in the school? Oh, Lady Mary, I would love to do that.'

My mouth was running away with me, but Lady Mary was giving me a funny look, so I stopped talking.

'I'm sorry if you misunderstood me, Lily,' she said.

'I was only joking,' I said with a forced laugh.

'I was going to suggest that one day you might like

to chat with Lady Georgina about the school,' she said. 'You know – learn a little bit about its history. She likes to talk about it.'

'That would be very interesting,' I said. 'Thank you, Lady Mary.'

Now I felt foolish. I wasn't a schoolgirl any more. No one wanted to praise me and say what I great girl I was. No one cared about my good work unless they were going to wear it or sleep on it.

This was very awkward and embarrassing. I didn't know what to say, and it looked as if Lady Mary was struggling too.

Suddenly she smiled. 'I have an idea,' she said. 'You know we have a home industries show in the riding school every summer?'

'No.' I didn't like to say that I didn't even know what a home industries show was, but maybe she guessed from the blank look on my face.

'It's a competition. People like yourself exhibit things.'

'What kind of things?'

'All kinds. They exhibit heads of cabbage, bunches of parsnips, pots of honey – that sort of thing.'

I didn't understand. 'But where would I get cabbage and parsnips? And if I did get them, I wouldn't be bringing them to a show, I'd be bringing them home to my mam for the dinner.'

Lady Mary laughed. 'That sounds very sensible to me. The vegetable categories are aimed at farmers – they are very competitive about that sort of thing, I believe. For you I was thinking of the sewing exhibits. There are competitions for the neatest embroidery and the best item of ladies clothing and the best child's dress, and more besides. There are prizes too – three shillings for first prize in every section.'

'Three shillings!' I forgot about my embarrassment as I thought of all the lovely things I could buy with three shillings. Then I put my head down. I didn't need another stupid dream that was never going to come true. How could my sewing be good enough

for such a competition? Where would I get the fabric and the threads?

But it was as if Lady Mary could read my mind. 'Your sewing is the neatest I have ever seen, Lily,' she said.

'But...'

'And in the cupboard under the attic stairs there are yards and yards of fabric that are never going to be used. Feel free to take whatever you wish. Actually, why don't you come with me now and choose something for your first project?'

I followed her along the corridor, and she opened a large cupboard I'd never noticed before. As Lady Mary had promised, the shelves were stacked high with fabric, all neatly folded.

'Oh, my,' I said, wondering what Mam would say if she could see so much fabric in one place.

Lady Mary pulled out a piece of yellow cotton. 'What do you think of that?' she asked.

'I ... I don't know what to think,' I said, as I stroked

it. 'It's so soft, and so beautiful.'

'Then it's yours. Perhaps you would like to make a child's dress first?'

'Of course, Lady Mary. Is it Miss Bridget you're thinking of? Will I make a dress for her?'

'That's very sweet of you, but Bridget has more dresses than she has days to wear them. I believe you have little sisters?'

I nodded.

'Well, then. Why not make some dresses for them – as practice? The show isn't until next August, so you have many months before you need something to submit.'

'Oh, Lady Mary!' I couldn't say any more. Already I could picture little Winnie and Anne's faces if I were to make them dresses from this fine fabric. They'd be the prettiest girls in the whole parish. I'd never actually made a whole dress before, but that was only a small detail. Mam could help me with the first one.

'Thank you so very much,' I whispered.

'You are most welcome – and please, help yourself to anything else you need from this cupboard – no need to ask. I will be very happy to see it put to good use. Now I will leave you, as Sir Josslyn and I are going to Sligo shortly.'

She had turned away when I remembered that I had something to say to her too.

'Lady Mary,' I said. 'There's one thing – about that Christmas present you generously said you would buy me.'

'Yes? You wanted a doll, didn't you? I haven't got it yet, I'm afraid.'

I couldn't help feeling disappointed. If she'd already bought it, then it would have been rude of me not to accept, but now I knew I had to do the sensible thing. I spoke quickly, not giving myself a chance to back out.

'It's just that ... I've changed my mind. A doll would have been very nice, but I realise now that what I really want is a pair of strong boots for the winter – if

201

that's all right with you.'

She looked carefully at me. 'Boots don't seem like a very exciting present for a girl of your age – and you were so sure that you wanted a doll.'

What could I say to that? Lady Mary was being nice, but she seemed a million miles away from me. Could she ever understand that poor girls like me were so different to her pampered darlings in the nursery? Didn't she see that I'd been confused between what I wanted and what I needed?

'I'm sure,' I said. 'Thank you very much.'

'As you wish. Now hold out your foot so I can see what size it is.'

I did as she asked. 'You look about the same size as me,' she said. 'And that will help me when I'm shopping. I'll buy you a nice pair of boots, I promise.'

'Thank you, Lady Mary,' I said, and I hurried away before she could see the tears in my eyes.

* * *

I was on my way downstairs after repairing the curtain when Maeve found me.

'Hello, Lily,' she said. 'It's painting time.'

We went to her room, and I put my sewing basket on the floor in the corner.

'Will I put on the blue dress again?' I asked, too nervous to even consider trying anything else.

'Actually I've changed my mind. I don't feel much like painting today.'

'Oh,' I said, feeling disappointed as I walked towards the door. 'I'd better go back downstairs. Mrs Bailey will—'

'No. Wait.'

'You've changed your mind again? That was quick.'

'I haven't changed my mind,' she said, laughing. 'Portrait painting isn't for me. I can see that now. Maybe another time I will try landscapes, or I might paint one of the horses. But you don't have to leave.'

'I think perhaps I do, Maeve. I would dearly love to

stay here all day chatting to you, but I'm not free like you are. I have work to do. If anyone discovers that you aren't painting, then I have no reason to be here.'

A sly smile came over her face. 'But I *might* do some painting, if the mood takes me. I'll set up the easel, and you can sit there in your usual place.'

I smiled too as I saw what she was doing. 'So, I'll just stay in my uniform then?'

'Yes. If I decide to paint, your uniform will do very well.'

So Maeve set up the easel and paper, picked up a paintbrush she had no intention of using, and we chatted happily for a long time.

Chapter Eighteen

*N*ext morning Nellie and I were tidying the drawing room as usual after breakfast. I was already tired after cleaning all the bedrooms and dressing rooms.

'I could cry,' I said, as I gathered up a bundle of newpapers. 'Every single day we tidy this room a couple of times, and as soon as we're finished, the family messes it up, and then we tidy it again – and again – and again. It seems like such a waste of time. If they kept the room tidy, you and I could have an extra twenty minutes in bed every morning.'

'So you'd like if the family kept every place tidy?' asked Nellie.

'Yes, wouldn't you?'

'Maybe not. If they didn't make a mess, we'd have no jobs. That might not be so bad for you, but if I had

to go back to the ...'

She didn't finish the sentence. I looked up and saw that there were tears in her eyes. Suddenly I understood something for the first time – Nellie was still terrified of being sent back to the workhouse. The fear was like a huge black cloud following her around. I was only working at Lissadell because Mam needed the money, but for Nellie, it was all she ever wanted, and she was afraid of losing it. I suppose everyone's dream is different.

'Oh, Nellie,' I said as I gave her a quick hug. 'You don't have to worry about going back to ... to that place. You're the best and most loyal worker in all of Lissadell. Even if anything happened that you had to leave – but I know it won't – you'd find another position in no time.'

'You think so?'

'I *know* so. I understand that you've had a terrible time, but that's over – forever. You've come so far, and who knows what wonderful things lie ahead for you?'

Suddenly Nellie gave a big smile, and I felt proud that I'd been able to cheer her up so easily.

'Dog!' she said.

'Where?' I asked, looking around. Had one of Sir Josslyn's dogs been in here all the time? If it was a hairy one that would mean extra work for Nellie and me. Then I realised she was looking at a newspaper I was carrying.

'Let me see,' she said, taking it from my hand. She lay the newspaper on the table, and pointed proudly at the word 'dog' in an advertisement.

'Look,' she said. 'I read the word by myself. I'm reading the newspaper.'

'So you are,' I said.

The she was sad again. 'But it's only one word. I bet you could read the whole paper from front to back.'

'Maybe,' I said, not wanting to boast that I'd been able to read the Master's newspaper since I was eight years old. 'And anyway, soon you'll be able to do the same. Here, I'll help you with this line. Read after

me: *Good hunting dog wanted.*'

Nellie was just starting to say the words when the door flew open. I quickly folded the newspaper, and the two of us stood there, looking guilty. Luckily it was only Maeve.

'There you are at last, Lily,' she said. 'I'm very bored today so I've come up with a plan. I thought the two of us could go to the beach.'

A day at the beach sounded very nice, except for a few problems. I was supposed to be working, and also it was December!

'I know it's December,' said Maeve, as if she could read my mind. 'But it's a lovely day and I'm fed up of being inside. I understand that you have work to do, but I've already spoken to Mrs Bailey and she says you may be excused. I need you to help me find a nice location for my first painting of the sea.'

I was getting to know how Maeve's mind worked, and I was fairly sure she had no intention of even thinking about painting, she just wanted someone

to spend time with. Once again I felt sorry for her. Even when she was with her granny and the rest of her family, there was something lonely about her, as if she were a bit lost, and didn't properly belong anywhere. Sometimes I wished that I could be rich like Maeve, but I wasn't sure that I'd actually like to swap lives with her.

'All right,' I said. 'Let's go to the beach.'

'Excellent. Have you been to Rosses Point before?'

Once Daddy borrowed a pony and trap to take our family to Rosses Point. Winnie was only a little baby, so she slept the whole day long, but the rest of us had the time of our lives. We swam in the sea and played in the sand dunes, and we had no dinner, but Mam brought bread and cake and lemonade for us and we ate until we thought we were going to burst. Even though it was summer, we didn't get home till dark, and Daddy had to carry the little ones to bed and in the morning Jimmy thought it had all been a dream. Daddy died a few months after that, so it was

a happy memory and a sad one all at the same time.

'Actually, yes I have been to Rosses Point, Maeve,' I said. 'But why are you asking me that?'

'Because that's where we're going.'

'But when you said we were going to the beach I thought you meant Lissadell Beach, the one at the end of the garden. Rosses Point is miles and miles away. Even if we start walking now ...'

'We're not walking all the way there, silly – we're going in the motor car. Now hurry up, Albert is bringing it round and I don't want to keep him waiting.'

I was so excited I wanted to jump up and down and scream. Me – in a motor car! This was the best thing that had ever happened to me. What would Denis and Jimmy say when they heard?

I turned to Nellie, but she was just standing there, holding her feather duster and looking like a statue of a housemaid. Her face was blank, but she can't have been very happy. If I were in her position, I think I would be nearly spitting with jealousy.

'Lily? Are you coming or not?' asked Maeve.

She sounded impatient, but I didn't know what to do. How could I go away leaving Nellie to do all the work on her own? How could I go on an adventure to the beach, when Nellie never went anywhere at all?

I took a deep breath and rushed the words out before I could change my mind.

'Maybe you could take Nellie out instead of me, Maeve. I'll go and tell Mrs Bailey, but I'm sure she won't mind, as long as one of us is here – and we've done the most important jobs already – and I can easily manage what's left.'

'But, Lily, you're the one I've invited,' said Maeve. 'Don't you want to come with me?'

'Of course I want to come,' I said. 'But ...'

'It's all right, Lily,' said Nellie. 'Don't worry about me. You go and have fun with Miss Maeve.'

I felt as if I was being torn in two. Nellie wasn't being mean or sarcastic – she really wanted me to

enjoy myself. She must have thought that life was very unfair, though, since I got so many things that seemed to be out of her reach.

I stared at Maeve, hoping she'd understand what was going on. 'Take Nellie with you to the beach,' I said. 'Please.'

I could see that Maeve was disappointed, and a little bit of me was happy about that – I was glad that she still saw me as her special friend. She wasn't pleased, but she couldn't say anything without insulting Nellie – and she was much too polite to do that.

'As you wish,' she said. 'We'd better all go down to Mrs Bailey and get this sorted out.'

Maeve skipped out the door while Nellie and I quickly gathered up the newspapers and our dusters and sweeping brushes. As we headed for the back stairs, I noticed that she was shaking all over. Was she excited, or was she terrified? I was trying to be nice, but maybe I had made a huge mistake.

'Are you happy about the day out, Nellie?' I asked.

'You're being so kind and I don't deserve it – I don't deserve any of it.'

'Of course you do,' I said. 'But are you happy?'

'I'm not sure. The thought of me going to the sea-side in a motor car … I'm happy about that … but what will I say to Miss Maeve? I'm not chatty like you. I'll say something stupid and she'll laugh at me … and …'

'Maeve is nice,' I said. 'She won't laugh at you.'

I couldn't say any more as now we were at the door of Mrs Bailey's study, where Maeve was waiting for us. She knocked, and a second later Mrs Bailey was standing in the doorway looking at us. 'Well, well,' she said, smiling at Maeve. 'A delegation – this must be important.'

'It is, Mrs Bailey,' said Maeve. 'You know I told you I was taking Lily out for the day? Well, she has suggested that I take Nellie instead, so I wanted to make sure that's all right with you.'

Mrs Bailey looked at the three of us for a long

time. Nellie was still shaking, and I was trying not to cry at the thought of the opportunity I'd just given up. I might live to be a hundred and never again have the chance to go in a motor car.

'Have you finished in the dining room and drawing room?' asked Mrs Bailey.

'Yes,' said Nellie and I together, though the drawing room hadn't had much of a going-over.

'I had hoped you girls would empty and tidy the linen press this afternoon,' she said.

'I can easily do that on my own,' I said quickly.

Mrs Bailey smiled. 'I'm sure you could, but I think perhaps the linen press can wait for another day.'

'So what would you like me to do instead?' I asked, hoping it wouldn't be something horrible and dirty like cleaning out the coal buckets.

'Miss Maeve, I presume there's room in that motor car for both Lily and Nellie?'

'Of course,' said Maeve. 'More than enough.'

I could hardly believe my ears.

'You mean we can both go?' I asked.

Mrs Bailey patted my shoulder. 'I think we can manage without you for one day. Delia can be spared from the kitchen if anything important comes up – and you and Nellie can work twice as hard tomorrow.'

This was a perfect solution. I could go on the trip, and both Maeve and Nellie would be happier with me there. I couldn't stop myself. I hugged Mrs Bailey and gave her a big kiss on the cheek.

She was embarrassed, but I think a little bit pleased too.

'You're only young once,' she said. 'Go and have a good time – and mind you have those girls back in time to light the bedroom fires tonight, Miss Maeve.'

'I promise,' said Maeve. 'Now Lily and Nellie, you go and get changed, and I'll see you in the *porte cochere* in ten minutes.'

Maeve went upstairs and Nellie ran along the corridor towards our room, but Mrs Bailey took my arm and held me back. Had she changed her mind

already?

'That's a very nice thing you tried to do for Nellie,' she said. 'You're a kind girl.'

'Thank you Mrs Bailey,' I said. Mam always says it's rude to boast about good things you do, but it's a lovely feeling when someone notices anyway. I sang a little song to myself as I skipped towards my room.

* * *

It didn't take me long to decide what to wear. I pulled my Sunday best dress from the press, and put it on. When I was ready, Nellie was still standing in the middle of the room, holding her only dress, a sad, limp-looking thing of faded grey cotton.

'I can't go in the motor car in this dress,' she said. 'Miss Maeve will feel ashamed to be seen with me.'

Maeve was a fine lady who didn't have to be ashamed of anything, but I knew that nothing I could say would make Nellie change her mind.

'Here,' I said, pulling my other dress from the press. 'Wear this – and no arguing or Maeve will go without us.'

When Nellie was dressed, I brushed her curly red hair and used one of my clips to hold it back from her face.

'You look beautiful,' I said. She smiled shyly and her cheeks went pink, and she looked like a lovely girl in a painting.

Then we both put on our winter coats and ran upstairs.

* * *

Nellie and I stood awkwardly in the *porte cochere*. Albert didn't notice us – he was busy polishing the bumpers, which were already so shiny I could see my face in them. I was afraid of touching anything – I didn't want to leave my fingerprints anywhere. I wondered if this whole thing was a very bad idea.

What business did girls like us have, going off in this big car?

I looked at Nellie, and was about to say that maybe we should go back inside, put on our uniforms and start tidying the linen press. The scared look on her face told me she wouldn't argue. Before I could say a word though, Maeve appeared and closed the front door behind her.

'This is so nice,' she said. 'We're going to have a lovely day, I simply know it.'

And when I heard those words, I knew I shouldn't be scared. So what if Maeve was wearing a fine cloak with a real fur collar, while Nellie's coat and mine were patched and worn? Maeve was a just girl like us, and we all deserved to have a nice time every now and then.

'All ready?' asked Albert, and when Maeve nodded, he opened the back door of the car and held it so Nellie and I could climb in. He might have been surprised to be driving two housemaids around, but he

was decent enough not to show it. Nellie and I sat back on the lovely black leather seats. Albert handed us each a thick rug to put over our knees, and then he closed the door.

Maeve climbed into the front seat, Albert started the engine and off we went.

Chapter Nineteen

At first I was absolutely terrified. The wind was blowing my hair all around my face, and I clung onto the side of the car with both hands, afraid that we'd go over a bump and we'd all fall out and die. I turned to look at Nellie, ready to give her one of my hands to hold, but she was laughing as if this was the most fun she'd ever had in her whole life. I'd never noticed before that she's much braver than I am.

Before long I got used to the wind and the noise and the bumping and I started to enjoy myself. I couldn't wait to tell Denis and Jimmy about this – but I wondered if they'd even believe me.

'How fast are we going?' I shouted.

Albert pointed at a dial on the front of the car. 'Fifteen miles an hour,' he said.

I'm quite good at arithmetic, but the numbers

didn't seem to make any sense. Fifteen miles in one hour is so fast – if I had a car of my own, I'd be able to go home to Mam for dinner every single day. (But I suppose if I was rich enough to own a car, I'd buy a fine house for Mam and we'd live there together and I'd never again have to be a housemaid.)

For a while no one said anything. I was happy to look at the countryside racing by, and watch the cows in the fields, who paid no attention to us at all, and didn't seem to care that I was having the most exciting day of my life.

After a while, Nellie began to sing. I'd never heard her sing before, and had no idea what a beautiful voice she had. I looked at her in surprise, but she just shrugged as if to tell me that there were lots of things about her that I didn't know. I'm not the best singer in the world, but I joined in anyway, and after a minute, so did Maeve and Albert, and we were a jolly group as we made our way along the road.

We were in Rosses Point in no time. Maeve, Nellie

and I climbed down from the motor car, and at first I felt a bit dizzy, as if I'd been on a roundabout. Maeve looked as if nothing much had happened, but Nellie was smiling so much I thought her face might crack.

'I have to run a few errands for Sir Josslyn,' said Albert. 'I'll see you young ladies back here at four o'clock. How does that sound?'

It sounded good to me, except I wondered how we were supposed to know when it was four o'clock.

Then Maeve pulled up the sleeve of her dress and I saw that she was wearing a beautiful wristwatch. 'Lucky I borrowed this from Aunt Mary, then, isn't it,' she said. 'Thank you, Albert. See you later.'

We watched as Albert drove away, and when he disappeared around a bend I felt a sudden sense of freedom.

'It's only ten to twelve,' said Maeve. We have more than four whole hours. What shall we do first?'

'Beach,' said Nellie and I together.

'Beach it is,' said Maeve. 'Let's go.'

* * *

For a minute I felt sad, as we walked along the track to the beach. Last time I'd walked along those stones I'd been holding my daddy's big warm hand, and now I missed him very much. But Daddy always loved singing and fun and games and I knew he'd want me to be happy, so I pushed the sad thoughts away and started to run towards the sea with my friends.

We took off our shoes and stockings and put them in a pile on the sand. Then we raced each other to the water's edge. Nellie was the first to hold up her skirt and paddle, jumping up and down with the shock of the cold. Maeve and I followed her and I gasped. The water was really and truly like ice wrapped around my feet, but it was fun, so we paddled for ages. I showed the girls how to skim stones, and we did that for a while, and then, when our feet were nearly blue from the cold, we came out of the water.

'Last one to that pile of stones is a rotten egg,'

said Nellie. I wondered who had taken my shy, prim friend and replaced her with this laughing girl, but I couldn't wonder for too long because she'd already started to run. The three of us got to the stones at the same time, and we collapsed onto the sand, breathless and laughing.

* * *

When we were rested, we went for a walk in the sand dunes. Nellie and I had put our sturdy boots back on, and Maeve didn't seem to care that her pretty shoes were getting ruined. It must be nice to have so many shoes that you need a special press to keep them in, and don't care if one pair is spoiled by the sand.

'You've got a beautiful singing voice, Nellie,' said Maeve, as we walked along.

'Thank you,' said Nellie. 'I love singing. I know lots of tunes, but I'd like to learn the words to more songs.'

'That's easy to arrange,' said Maeve. 'There are lots

of song books in my house at Ardeevin. I'll get a few for you next time I go there.'

I stopped walking. Poor Nellie – this was so embarrassing for her. What was she going to do now?

'That's very kind of you,' she said. 'But I wouldn't want you to waste your time. You see, I'm not very good at reading, and I could never read the big words in a song book. Lily is teaching me though, and maybe one day……'

'I'm sorry, Nellie. I didn't realize,' said Maeve. 'Let me know when you're ready and I'll bring some books for you.'

Then she ran ahead of us along a narrow path.

'That must have been hard for you, Nellie,' I said. 'Telling Maeve about your reading.'

'Not really.' I was surprised, remembering how she had tried to keep the truth from me, but then she continued. 'I used to think I was stupid, but since you've been teaching me, and I've learned so much, I know that's not true. None of this is my fault. If you'd

been my teacher all along, I'd probably be the best reader in Ireland by now.'

I smiled. My dream of being a teacher might never come true, but in one small way I had changed Nellie's life.

* * *

When we caught up with Maeve, she was kneeling behind a big grassy mound.

'Shhh,' she whispered. 'It's a baby hare.'

We crouched next to her and saw the tiny creature sitting in the middle of an open patch of grass.

'What's it doing out there all on its own?' I said. 'It won't stand a chance if a fox or a bird decides it wants it for its dinner.'

'You're right,' said Maeve. 'It might be hurt, and we have to help it.'

The three of us walked towards the tiny animal. It blinked its huge brown eyes at us, but it didn't move,

and we knew it must be injured somehow.

'Pick it up, Lily,' said Maeve.

It was only tiny, but I was afraid. 'You pick it up,' I said, but Maeve didn't move either.

'I'll do it,' said Nellie as she bent down and picked up the hare. It was like a small bundle of fur, with its long ears pressed down towards its brown, speckled back.

I stroked it gently, and noticed that it was trembling. For a second I felt angry at the fine gentlemen who came to Lissadell to shoot poor little animals like this. What chance did they have against grown up men with guns?

'We have to find a safe place to leave it,' said Nellie. So we went to where the grass grew thickly, and Maeve pulled out handfuls to make a safe hollow for the tiny creature.

'Be a good little hare, and rest there until you feel better,' said Nellie as she lay the hare in its new home.

'And stay away from Uncle Josslyn and his hollow

cow,' said Maeve as we walked away.

'What on earth do you mean?' I asked.

Maeve giggled. 'Didn't you know? Uncle J has made himself a life-size model of a cow. He puts it in a field and hides himself inside it, so he can shoot unsuspecting birds and animals who come near him.'

I felt sorry for the poor birds and other animals, but the thought of the serious Sir Josslyn climbing inside the fake cow was hilarious.

'Does he bring a fake bear when he goes to the Arctic?' I asked. 'And when he goes to Africa, he could bring a fake elephant, which would be grand as there'd be room for all his friends too.'

Maeve laughed for a long time. 'You're so funny,' Lily,' she said.

I smiled. I was glad that Nellie was with us, and having a good time, but I was glad too that Maeve still liked me the best.

* * *

'I should have asked cook to make us a picnic,' said Maeve. 'I'm starving.'

I was starving too, and four o'clock seemed very far away. In summer and autumn I'm good at finding berries and nuts in the woods, but in December, on a beach ...

'We'll just have to find a tea-room,' said Maeve casually.

Nellie and I looked at each other. A tea-room is all very well for rich people like Maeve, but Nellie and I didn't have any money. (And even if I'd brought money with me, how could I spend my precious wages on fine food?)

'My treat,' said Maeve. 'Come along. I can't have you starving to death – Mrs Bailey would never forgive me.'

I don't like taking charity, but I don't like being hungry either, so I took Nellie's arm and we followed Maeve into the village.

The tea-room was very pretty, with linen tablecloths and fine china on all the tables. The only other customer was a man in a corner, reading a newspaper. I read the headline and saw that it was about the hungry strikers in Dublin. I wanted to tell him that Maeve's mam was the famous Countess Markievicz, who was probably at that minute peeling carrots and turnips to make soup for the poor children. I knew Maeve wouldn't like that though, so I kept my mouth shut.

The waitress showed us to a table, and took our coats. I was embarrassed at how shabby mine was, but the waitress didn't seem to notice or care.

When we were comfortably seated, she came back with a menu for each of us. Nellie opened hers and looked at it for a long time.

'I can see the word "tea",' she said proudly. 'And

look, there it is again.'

Maeve leaned over, and helped her to read another few words, and Nellie beamed when she read a whole line all by herself. I couldn't concentrate on the words though – all I could see were the prices. What would Mam say if she thought people paid this much for tea and little bits of food?

Should Nellie and I just order the cheapest thing on the menu to eat? If we asked for a glass of water, would Maeve have to pay for that?

'Will I order for us all?' suggested Maeve.

Nellie and I nodded gratefully, and ten minutes later, the waitress came back with a huge tray, piled up with food. We had tiny sandwiches filled up with cheese and fish paste, with no crusts at all on the bread, and cream buns and pretty little cakes with pink and blue icing on the top. We ate until we were fit to burst, and then Maeve paid, using coins from a lovely silk purse she took from the pocket of her dress.

At the door, the waitress held my coat for me so

I could put my arms into it. She smiled at me, and didn't seem to mind that I was a housemaid pretending to be a fine lady for a day. She was nice.

* * *

We walked up and down the street for a while, talking about this and that and looking into the windows of the few small shops. Nellie's fingers were cold, so Maeve lent her her own gloves, and Nellie didn't say a word for ages as she looked at the fine, soft leather, and held it to her face.

When we got to the place we were to meet Albert at four o'clock, there was no sign of him or the car, and Nellie began to worry.

'What if Albert doesn't come back for us?' she said. 'What if the car has broken down?'

'Don't worry,' said Maeve. 'He'll be along shortly.'

Nellie still looked worried, and I have to admit that I was a bit concerned too. Maeve just sat on a stone

wall and hummed a little tune, and then I realised the biggest difference between us. Nellie and I had to worry about Mrs Bailey and Mr Kilgallon and all the jobs waiting for us back at Lissadell. Maeve only had to worry about herself.

Five minutes later we heard the sweet sound of a motor car coming towards us, and ten minutes after that we were on the road home. We'd only been gone for a few hours, but I felt as if I had been on the longest holiday a girl could ever have.

* * *

'That was the best day of my whole life,' said Nellie as we got ready for bed. 'If I die tonight, I'll die a happy girl.'

'Don't die!' I said. 'I'll never manage all the extra work without you tomorrow.'

We laughed for a minute, and then I fell asleep, and had long, long dreams of running on the sand with my friends.

Chapter Twenty

a week before Christmas, Mrs Bailey said we had to get every bedroom in the house ready for guests.

'Lissadell will be on show,' she said. 'And we cannot let Sir Josslyn and the family down. We will all have to do our very best work.'

Easy for her to say! All she had to do was stand in her office with a long face and a bundle of lists, while Nellie and I and the other maids had to run around like mad things, trying to get everything done on time. Every bed had to be shaken out and made up with fresh sheets. Every carpet had to be beaten and every surface had to be dusted. The furniture had to be polished until we could see our faces in it, and the windows had to be cleaned with newspapers and vinegar.

A few times Maeve found me and brought me to her room, where she pretended to paint, and I sewed the dress I was making for Winnie. I knew Maeve was lonely, and I loved those quiet moments with her – and was very glad of the rest, too. The thought of everyone else working so hard though, made me feel guilty, and I always left before long.

Nellie and I tried to continue our lessons, but when bedtime came, we were both practically asleep on our feet, so in the end we agreed that we'd take a holiday from lessons until Christmas was over.

I was exhausted by the time visitors started arriving, three days before Christmas. Some came in motor cars and some in fancy carriages. All afternoon I heard wheels on the driveway, and whenever I could, I rushed to look over the bannisters. I loved seeing the ladies in their silk and satin gowns, the men in their fine suits, and the darling little children with their ribbons and bows. I began to think that all the hard work had been worth it.

Later, though, I realized that having visitors isn't any fun when you're the one who has to take care of them. I was run off my feet, carrying towels upstairs, and straightening beds that had been lain on for less than ten minutes.

When supper time finally came, I was in for another surprise. I'd noticed that some visitors had brought their own servants with them, and of course they had to eat with us in the servants' hall. I thought it would be nice to see a few new faces, and was interested to hear what these new people would have to say about the Big Houses they worked in. Unfortunately, not all of the Lissadell staff saw it that way. I'd got used to the strict order in the way we sat at the table, but the new arrivals messed everything up. Some of them worked for people with higher titles than Sir Josslyn, so they thought they should sit higher up the table because of this. There were lots of rows, and even a bit of pushing and bad language. In the end, Mr Kilgallon had to shout to get everyone quiet, and

he gave us a fierce look that the Lissadell staff knew too well, and everyone settled down.

I caught Nellie's eye and we both giggled. I didn't really mind who was next to me, as long as it was someone nice I could chat with, like Maggie or Nellie. Some people at the table looked as if they had been deeply insulted, though, and wouldn't ever get over it as long as they lived.

* * *

The next day when I was sweeping the front hall, Maeve came racing down the stairs as if she were being chased by a pack of wild dogs. I looked up, wondering if she needed help with something, but she ran right past me.

'Mother is here!' she said. 'Mother is here at last!'

She opened the hall door, and a second later I saw the famous Countess Markievicz for the first time. She was coming up the steps, holding a beautiful

spaniel in her arms.

'Now, Poppet,' she said. 'Here we are. Home at last.'

She was tall and so, so elegant. She was wearing a heavy wool cloak over a blue velvet dress, and her hair was tied up with curls and ribbons. I thought she looked like a beautiful queen.

Maeve ran over, and stood quietly next to her, looking a little shy.

'Maeve, darling,' said the Countess, as she kissed her on both cheeks. For a second I felt sad for Maeve. If my mam hadn't seen me for months, she'd have hugged the life out of me and then hugged me a second time, just to make sure I was real.

The Countess put the dog down, and it promptly ran out the door towards the gardens.

The Countess handed her cloak to one of the footmen, while I stood quietly to the side, trying not to be a nuisance. For a moment, I thought Maeve might introduce us, that she might tell her mother about the painting, and the exciting day we'd had at the

seaside, but it was as if Maeve had forgotten that I was even there. They went into the drawing room, and closed the door behind them, and I continued with my sweeping.

* * *

On Christmas Eve, rich people came from all over the county for a big ball at Lissadell. Even though extra kitchen staff had been brought in, poor Cook looked as if she was going to die, she was working so hard.

Nellie and I and the other housemaids had to carry trays into the dining room, and my back was nearly broken from standing still and proper, waiting for the footmen to take whatever we were carrying, and put it on the plates from the warming cupboard. I had never seen so much food in all my life. The sideboards were piled up with turkeys and hams and spiced beef and even a boar's head with an orange in

its mouth!

When everyone was served, the footmen stood with their backs to the guests. Luckily there was a big mirror over the sideboard, so the head footman could see if Sir Josslyn or anyone else wanted something. I thought that was a very strange thing, but I didn't worry about it for long. I took my opportunity to go down to the kitchen and rest my sore feet for a while.

Later there was music and dancing, and again I had to stand at the side of the room holding a tray of drinks. I liked looking at the women swirling around, with their dresses floating along the floor. All the women looked like angels, but Countess Markievicz and her sister Lady Eva, were the most beautiful of all. Maeve once told me that a famous poet wrote a poem about them and said that Lady Eva was like a gazelle. I didn't know what that was, but I liked the word, and guessed it was a good thing to be like one. I could see that the two sisters were best friends and for much of the night, they

were huddled in a corner, chatting.

* * *

It must have been nearly dawn by the time Nellie and I got to bed, and a short hour or two later it was time for us to get up again. I was sad, thinking how I'd like be at home with Mam and the little ones, all ready for a lovely long Christmas day together.

Nellie came and sat on my bed. 'I know you'd prefer to be at home,' she said.

Now I wanted to cry. How could she feel sorry for me, when she had no home to go to at all?

Then she handed me something small. I unwrapped the brown paper and found a soft cotton hankie, trimmed with lace. Embroidered on a corner were the words *'for my good friend.'*

'Oh, Nellie,' I said. 'That's beautiful.'

She went red. 'I made it myself, using bits of the sheets that couldn't be mended any more – and Mrs

Bailey gave me some lace she'd saved from one of Miss Bridget's old dresses and Isabelle showed me how to do the words.'

Hanora and Rose and I had never exchanged presents so I hadn't thought to get anything for Nellie. Then I remembered my last trip home. Mam had hugged me at the door as usual, and then ran back inside.

'Before you go I have to give you your Christmas present,' she said when she came back. 'And I made a little something for Nellie too, since she has no mam to make her anything at all.'

Now I got the two parcels from under my bed.

'These are from Mam,' I said.

Nellie's eyes opened wide. 'Can I watch you opening them?'

'You can watch me opening one of them,' I said.

'I understand,' said Nellie. 'I'll go and wash myself while you are opening the other one.'

I laughed. '*You'll* be opening the other one. Mam

sent it for you.'

Nellie gasped. 'Your mam sent a present for me? But she doesn't even know me.'

Now I felt awkward, wondering if she'd be offended. 'I told her a little bit about you – that you're my friend, and that ... anyway, this one is yours.'

Nellie took the present in her hand and looked at it for a long time, as if she could hardly believe her eyes. Out in the corridor, I could hear the other maids hurrying towards the stairs.

'Nellie,' I whispered. 'I'd love this moment to last forever, but if we don't get to work quickly, Mrs Bailey will ...'

Nellie tore off the paper and I saw a pair of mittens in the grey wool Mam used for nearly everything, but trimmed with pink and yellow ribbons. Nellie put on the mittens and held her hands out.

'No one has ever made anything especially for me before,' she whispered. 'Every stitch I've ever owned was worn by someone else first. I will treasure these

always. Thank you, Lily.'

'Mam will be glad you liked them,' I said.

I just had time to take a quick look at my present from Mam. It was a beautiful blouse in soft blue fabric that I knew was once part of Mam's Sunday dress. I held it to my face, and smelled the familiar smell of turf smoke. My chest hurt as I thought of Mam cutting up her best thing, so I could have a Christmas present. Tears rolled down my face as I thought how much I'd love to be waking up in my own little house with my mam and my brothers and sisters. Nellie cried too, but I don't know if she was crying for me, or thinking about all the Christmases she'd never have with her own family.

Just then there was a knock at the door, and I heard Maggie's voice. 'I know it's Christmas, she said. 'But Mrs Bailey is fit to kill the two of you. Hurry along or she will surely have a conniption.'

Nellie and I wiped our eyes and our Christmas day began.

Chapter Twenty-one

The servants' dinner was very good that day, with turkey and ham for everyone, and lemonade and cakes and treats afterwards. Just as we were finished eating, I noticed that people were standing up, which was strange, as Mrs Bailey hadn't said it was time to go back to work. Then I saw that Sir Josslyn and Lady Mary had come into the room, followed by two of the footmen whose arms were filled with presents, all wrapped up in shiny paper.

'Happy Christmas, everyone,' said Lady Mary. 'Please sit down, and we will distribute your gifts.'

Suddenly the room was full of excited whispers, though I wasn't sure why at first, as everyone already knew what they were getting. I suppose in a world where we didn't get many presents, even a not-surprise one was very welcome.

When my turn came I was excited too. Lady Mary gave me my present, and Sir Josslyn reached out to shake my hand, but I couldn't do it because my hands were full already, and I forgot to say thank you, and I got all confused and dropped the present, but no one minded or laughed or anything. We were all just very happy.

I carefully unwrapped my present, folding up the shiny paper for Mam, who I knew would treasure it. They were the most beautiful boots I had ever seen – soft, smooth leather the colour of ripe conkers, and thick, strong soles that would last for years. They were perfect, but I still felt a moment of sadness as I thought of the sweet doll that would never be mine. Then I watched as everyone else unwrapped jackets and shoes and hats and I realised that if I'd got a doll, it would have looked very strange indeed.

I admired Nellie's warm winter jacket, and Maggie's soft shawl, and soon Lady Mary and Sir Josslyn went back upstairs. A few minutes later, Mrs Bailey

and Mr Kilgallon stood up, giving the rest of us the signal that it was time to go back to our jobs. Christmas is all very good and well, but when you're a servant there's always work to do.

* * *

After supper that night, I was so tired, I was fit to fall down and die. I thought I might have a moment to rest, but Mrs Bailey had a different idea.

'Lily, the bedroom fires need to be seen to. Take some coal upstairs right now.'

I filled the coal bucket and slowly made my way up the back stairs. Half way up, I stopped to rest. I was still rubbing my aching back when I heard footsteps behind me. Too tired to turn around, I wondered which of the servants it was, and if they were likely to help me. Then I heard a voice that definitely didn't come from a servant's mouth.

'You poor child. That coal bucket is nearly as big

as yourself.'

It was Countess Markievicz! I had no time to wonder what she was doing on the back stairs, as I tried to move the bucket out of her way. In my rush, it tipped over, and in horror, I watched as the coal tumbled out and down the stairs like a big dirty black waterfall.

'I'm so sorry, Countess,' I said, as she jumped out of the way. 'Are you all right? Did you get dirty? I didn't mean ...'

I was terrified, and wondering if this was to be my last day at Lissadell, but she was laughing. 'Please,' she said. 'Call me Madame. And don't worry at all – a few lumps of coal never killed anyone.'

'Thank you, Cou— I mean Madame.' I straightened the bucket, and scrambled to pick up the coal.

'Here, let me help you.'

How could I let a real live Countess help me with the dirty coal? But before I could answer, she took off her long satin gloves, and began to pick up the lumps

with her bare hands.

I know I wasn't supposed to speak without being spoken to, but I felt I had to break the rules.

'No, Madame, please. Let me do it.'

As if she didn't hear me, she continued to gather up the coal and toss it into the bucket. She was bigger and faster than me, so in the end she had done most of the work. Then she picked up the bucket as if it was as light as a feather, and headed upstairs.

'For the bedrooms, I presume?' she said as I hurried after her.

'Madame, please don't,' I said. 'Let me carry it.'

'But you're only a slip of a girl. It's much too heavy for you.'

She was right, but no one else seemed to care about that.

'I have to do it every day,' I said. 'I'm nearly used to it by now.'

She stopped and smiled at me, and suddenly I felt shy.

'I've carried plenty of coal in my time,' she said. 'And in more difficult circumstances than this, I can tell you. You wouldn't believe your ears if I told you half of what I have seen in the tenements of Dublin.'

I could hardly believe this was happening to me. A real live Countess was talking to me, and telling me a little bit about her exciting life. I wanted to stay on that narrow stairs all night, listening to her stories, but then I heard Mrs Bailey calling Nellie from the corridor at the bottom of the stairs, and I remembered who I was.

'Please, Madame,' I said. 'Let me take the bucket. I'll get in trouble if anyone sees you.'

The Countess ran up the last few steps and when she got to the door at the top of the stairs she put down the bucket. 'I didn't think about that,' she said. 'How silly of me. Do you think you can manage from here?'

'Yes, thank you.'

'Very well then, good night.'

And I watched as the finest lady I'd ever seen, with a stain on her fancy dress and a black smudge on her face, opened the door and walked along the corridor in front of me, whistling as she went.

* * *

After a while, I feared that the visitors were never going to leave. I was bored of looking at all the fine dresses, and I was definitely fed up of making beds and lighting fires. The days seemed to go on forever, and there was never time to laugh with the other servants or do my sewing or continue Nellie's lessons. Any time I saw Maeve, she was with her mother, or running along with her English cousins. She always gave me a friendly smile, but I knew that while the visitors were there, she'd have no time for me. It didn't seem fair, but there wasn't any reason to blame her. She wasn't the one who made the rules saying that our lives had to be so different.

One day I went into the kitchen and Cook was singing as she worked.

'You're happy, Cook,' I said. 'I haven't heard you singing for more than a week.'

She smiled at me. 'I'm very happy. You know the family and all the guests are invited to a ball in a Big House near Sligo this evening?'

'Of course I know,' I said. 'Who do you think had to carry all the extra towels and soap up to the dressing rooms earlier on?'

'You?'

I nodded. 'And who do you think had to spend hours mending dresses and sewing on buttons and turning up hems?'

'You again, I suppose, and I'm sorry for all your extra work, pet, but it's good news for me. No fancy dinner for me to cook tonight. I only have to feed the servants, and there's lots of leftovers to be getting on with.'

'And after that there's the servants' party,' said

Maggie, who'd just come into the kitchen with a bundle of sheets in her arms.

'Party?' I said. 'No one told me anything about a party.'

'I presume everyone has been too busy to mention it,' said Cook. 'We've all been run off our feet these last weeks. Or maybe they thought you knew about it already.'

'But it's the best night of the whole year,' said Maggie.

And she was right!

It didn't matter that we were eating leftovers – the food that Cook served that night was the finest I'd ever eaten. She saw me sneaking two pastries for Winnie and Anne into the pocket of my apron. I could feel my face going red, but she came over and whispered in my ear.

'You eat up,' she said. 'And enjoy it. I have some treats put away for you to bring to your family.'

Everything tasted so nice, I didn't stop eating until

I was fit to burst. With no bells ringing from upstairs, everyone was more relaxed than I'd ever seen them, and there was lots of laughing and chat.

When the meal was over, the table was pushed to one side. One of the footmen played the fiddle, and another accompanied him on the spoons.

'Now who'll sing a song for us?' said Mrs Bailey. A stable boy stood up, but then Mrs Bailey continued, 'but there will be no rude songs in this kitchen as long as I'm alive.' The poor boy sat down again with a big red face, and I felt sorry for him.

And then Nellie stood up. 'I'll sing,' she said. Everyone looked surprised, including Nellie herself, almost as if she couldn't believe she'd actually said the words. She whispered to the fiddle player, and then she sang a sad song about a poor old woman who had to travel the roads begging. Next she sang a slow love song, and after that she sang a happy song that had everyone tapping their feet and clapping their hands. Even though everyone begged for more, she stopped

254

singing and came and sat beside me.

'You have such a beautiful voice,' I said. 'Why don't you sing every single day?'

'Why don't you ask me to?' she said with a grin, and all of a sudden I wanted to hug her. How had this gorgeous girl been hiding inside the cross person I had first known?

After that there was dancing, and I got so excited I jumped up on the table and danced a whole jig and a reel, and my new boots shone in the firelight, and everyone cheered me on, even Mrs Bailey.

The party continued until we heard the first motor car pull up outside the house.

Mr Kilgallon and the footmen straightened their clothes and went upstairs, while the rest of us scurried towards our beds.

'Those songs you sang were so lovely,' I said to Nellie, as we put out the light. 'How did you learn them?'

'There wasn't much singing in the workhouse, but

I learned a few songs when I came here. I had to pick up the words by listening, of course, but when I can read, I'm going to learn every single song in Miss Maeve's books.'

'Sounds like a good idea,' I said, sleepy after the long day and night.

'When I can read, I'm going to learn all kinds of things,' she said. 'My life is going to be so much better and it's all thanks to you.'

And that, I realised, was probably the best Christmas present I was ever going to get.

Chapter Twenty-two

In January I had two special days off, to make up for all the extra work at Christmas. Cook remembered her promise and gave me a big basket full of treats for the family.

I couldn't resist kissing her floury cheek. 'No one in my family has ever met you,' I said. 'But they all love you to bits.'

'Ah, get away with you,' she said, but I knew she was pleased.

I was excited as I ran to the drawing room to say goodbye to Nellie. She was singing to herself as she dusted the side tables.

'I can help you with that if you like,' I said.

'Absolutely not,' she said, pushing me away with a smile. 'It's your time off and I want you to enjoy every single minute with your family.'

We were great friends by now, and even though I was looking forward to seeing Mam and the little ones, I knew I'd miss Nellie while I was away.

'Lily?' she said, when I was nearly at the door.

'What?'

'I've been wanting to say. I mean ... you see ... there's something ... it's been bothering me ... so ...'

Her face was all red, and I was beginning to think that my two days off would be over before she finished her sentence.

'You can tell me anything,' I said, trying to hurry her along.

'You've always been nice to me,' she said.

'That's what friends do.'

'But when you first came here – I was mean to you.'

I couldn't really argue with her – she had been horrible in the beginning.

'That's all right,' I said.

'No, it's not all right. On your first day, and lots of days after that, I was very cruel and now I'm so sorry.

You see, I was afraid ... I was afraid that ...'

Even from all the way across the huge room, I could see the tears in her eyes. I came close to her and held her hand.

'What were you afraid of, Nellie?'

'I had two friends when I was in the ... in the work-house. Christina and Nora ... and they were so kind to me, they were the ones who made my life bearable. But one day Nora's aunt came to claim her ... and I was happy for Nora because she was getting away from that terrible place ... but my heart was breaking in two. I never saw Nora again.'

I could feel tears coming to my own eyes, as I tried to imagine what Nellie's pain must have been like.

'And Christina?' I asked, half afraid to hear the answer.

'It was a very hard winter ... and Christina got sick and she coughed all day and all night long ... there was no medicine ... I couldn't do anything to help her ... and she died ... and I was so sad I thought I would

die myself. And after that ... I was afraid ...'

At last I understood. 'Losing Christina and Nora was so awful, you were afraid to have any more friends after that?'

Nellie nodded. 'I didn't want to take the chance – I didn't want to feel that pain again – but all the time when I was here – I looked at the other servants chatting and laughing together – and I was so lonely – and then you came along – and you were so nice to me – but I was afraid ... if I became close to you ...'

'I understand,' I said. 'Sometimes it can be hard, but we all need friends – and now you've got me – whether you like it or not.'

Nellie smiled, and I used the corner of my shawl to wipe away first her tears and then my own.

'I really can stay and help you for a little bit,' I said. 'Mam won't mind if I'm a bit late, since I'll be with her for two whole days.'

'I won't hear of it,' she said, standing up tall. 'You go and have a nice time with your family, and I will

see you tomorrow, and you can tell me all about it.'

* * *

As I was coming out of the drawing room, I met Lady Mary.

'Ah, Lily, the very girl,' she said. 'I've been looking for you.'

'Is there something you want me to mend?' I asked, hoping she'd say 'no'. She'd never had a job in her life – how could she understand how important days off were to people like me?

'Please come along to my study, won't you?'

Suddenly I felt guilty about the basket of food under my arm. Cook had said it was leftovers, and I hoped Lady Mary would see it the same way. What if she thought I was stealing it? As I followed her, the basket felt like a sack of rocks, and I wished I could hide it away under one of the many tables and dressers that lined the corridor.

In her study, Lady Mary sat at her writing desk. I put the basket down on the rug and stood in front of her with my hands behind my back, the way Mrs Bailey had taught me. I looked down at my shiny new boots and waited for Lady Mary to speak.

'I've been very pleased with your work, Lily,' she said. 'I want you to know that I believe your sewing is particularly good.'

'Thank you, Lady Mary.'

'I was just in the nursery, and I thought of you.'

My heart sank. Was there lots of sewing waiting upstairs for me? I could mend nearly anything by now, but not on my precious days off.

'Yes, Lady Mary?'

She leaned behind her and picked something up from the floor. For a second I didn't understand what I was seeing – it was just like Miss Bridget's doll, the one I wanted so badly – except this one had golden red curls that reminded me a little bit of Nellie.

What was going on?

Was Lady Mary teasing me?

'I was sorry when you changed your mind about your Christmas present,' she said. 'I loved to play with dolls when I was your age, but I understand that you had to be practical.'

'The boots are very nice, thank you,' I said. 'They are the most comfortable boots I have ever owned.' (And also the first pair that hadn't been stretched by the feet of many others before me.)

'Bridget received far too many presents at Christmas,' she said. 'Her Aunt Mabel gave her this doll, which seems such a waste, as she has several exactly like it already.'

Did I dare to hope?

'I would not like Bridget to grow up spoiled. I would like her to be a decent girl like you.'

Was she saying ...?

'Which is why I would like you to have this doll.'

I could hardly breathe. 'But Miss Bridget, the poor little girl, I wouldn't want her to ...'

Lady Mary smiled. 'Trust me. She is but a baby, and she has so many dolls, she won't even miss this one.'

'I could mind it for her until she's older,' I said, trying to make myself feel better for taking the doll from the little child.

Lady Mary held the doll towards me. 'It's yours,' she said. 'To keep forever, and there's an end to the matter.'

'Thank you so very much, Lady Mary,' I said. 'I will call her Julianne and I will treasure her always.'

Then I picked up my basket, sat the doll on top of it and left.

* * *

It was a cold day, and I was glad of my warm boots for the long walk – and glad they actually fitted me too. I hummed to myself as I walked along. I hadn't been home for weeks, and I was so excited I thought

I'd burst.

I wondered if Winnie was well, and if Anne was still learning her letters.

Were the boys fighting and driving Mam mad?

Was a few weeks long enough for them to forget all about me?

But I needn't have worried. Winnie and Anne were waiting at the door, and when they saw me coming along the lane they raced to meet me. Clever Anne spotted Julianne immediately.

'A dolly,' she said, jumping up and down. 'You got a dolly. Can I see? Can I hold her?'

'Me, me,' said Winnie. 'Me hold dolly.'

'You can both hold her,' I said. 'You can take turns, but you have to be very careful. We don't want her to break, do we?

I put the basket down in the lane and handed the doll to each of my sisters in turn. Neither said anything as they held her as carefully as if she were a real baby. Their eyes were shining and they were smiling

so much I thought their little faces might crack. I wished I was rich enough to buy them all the dolls in the whole world.

* * *

When I got inside, Mam hugged me for a long time.

'My girl,' she kept saying as she stroked my hair. 'My darling girl is back.'

Denis and Jimmy weren't interested in the doll, but they dived into the basket as if it were full of gold and silver and jewels. They both pounced on a piece of sweet cake.

'It's mine,' said Denis. 'I touched it first.'

'But I saw it first so that means it's mine, doesn't it Mam?'

Mam let me go with a big sigh. 'None of ye will get a crumb if ye don't stop fighting right this minute.'

The boys dropped the cake and stood there sulking. I laughed – it was good to know that some things

would never change.

* * *

The day went very quickly. The little ones showed me the things Mam had made them for Christmas. Winnie sang a song that Jimmy had taught her, and Anne read out all the letters from her copybook.

In the evening time we went to Carty's house for a singsong. I handed a piece of cheese from Lissadell to Molly, the woman of the house, and she looked about ready to faint.

'Mercy me,' she said patting her chest as if she were checking to see that her heart was still in there under all her layers of shawls and blouses. 'Such a treat, and from the Big House – I don't know if we'll dare to eat it at all at all.'

'Well, if you're not going to eat it, then give it back,' said Anne reaching out her hand, and everyone laughed except for Mam who looked as if she wanted

to die from embarrassment.

* * *

It was late when we got home. Mam was sparing the candles so we got changed in the dark.

'I've been sleeping in your place on the outside of the bed, Lily,' said Denis. 'But you can have it back – just for tonight.'

'Thank you, Denis,' I said. I was glad he couldn't see me smiling in the darkness. My little brother used to fight me for everything – when had he become so grown-up?

Soon we were all settled in our usual places, with Winnie snuggled up next to me, twisting my hair around her fingers the way she always used to. Mam came to tuck us in, leaning across the bed to kiss everyone on the cheek.

'Sleep well, my little one,' she said to each of us in turn.

'Thank you, Mam,' I whispered. 'You sleep well too.'

It was strange to be back in my own bed, the one I'd slept in since I was tiny. I listened to the familiar sounds – Mam getting ready for bed and Winnie's snuffly breathing. Even though I was safe in my own little house, with my family all around me, I couldn't help feeling lonely. I wished for a life where I'd be sleeping with my brothers and sisters night after night. I wanted to go back to the days when Mam did all the worrying for me. I wanted my biggest problem to be who I'd sit beside in school next day. I wanted to be a little girl again.

But then Denis started to kick me, and Anne cried for a drink of water, and Winnie climbed on top of me and I could hardly breathe, and I remembered that nothing was perfect.

Chapter Twenty-three

'You ou should run along to Hanora's house and say hello,' said Mam after breakfast next morning. 'Who knows when you'll see her again?'

'I'll see her next Saturday, won't I?'

'Oh my poor little pet,' she said. 'I forgot you didn't know. The money for her ticket arrived last week. She leaves for America on Friday. Her poor mam and dad – they'll have neither chick nor child when she's gone. Maybe all they'll ever have from now on will be letters and money and photographs of fat American babies in pretty lace dresses.'

'When's the wake?' I asked.

'It's on Thursday night, so I'm afraid you'll be missing it – I'm sorry for that.'

I'm not sure that I was sorry. American wakes were usually fun, but how could I bear to be at a party,

when my friend was leaving? How could I dance and sing and eat sweet cake knowing that within a few hours Hanora would be on a ship, sailing far away from me?

'I'll go and see her now,' I said. 'And I'll be back in time for dinner.'

*   *   *

Hanora and I went for a walk along the lane. We'd been friends all our lives, but now I couldn't think of anything to say. As we strolled along in silence, I became sadder and sadder. Soon Rose would be leaving for Sligo and everything would be changed forever. New girls would be sitting in the big desks at school, and helping the Master with the little children. Miss O'Brien would be giving her special smile to someone else. In time, no one would remember that Hanora and Rose and I had ever been there, and when they saw my name scratched on the corner

desk they would have no idea who I was.

The lane is where Hanora and Rose and I gathered wild strawberries in summer, and searched for blackberries and crab apples when the chilly autumn winds were blowing. This was where we hid when we were trying to get away from our mams who needed us to do jobs.

'Remember the day William's goat escaped?' said Hanora.

'I'll never forget it,' I said. 'We chased him across five fields before we caught him. Rose's dress got torn, and I lost my best hair ribbon.'

'And you thought William would give us a reward for bringing him back.'

Now I could hardly talk I was laughing so much. 'And instead of giving us a reward, he chased us away with a stick, and blamed us for letting the goat out in the first place – which was so unfair.'

'Lily, there's one thing I never told you about that day.'

'What?'

'Well actually I might have opened the gate a little bit.'

'You what?' Hanora rarely did anything wrong, and I could hardly believe what I was hearing.

'I thought it would be fun, but that goat was a faster runner than I expected, and by the time he got to the third field, I didn't want to tell you what really happened.'

'So it was all your fault?'

'Yes,' she said, looking embarrassed. 'I'm sorry.'

'Don't be sorry,' I said. 'That was the funniest afternoon of my life. When I'm an old woman with a bad back and creaky bones I'll still remember how the three of us laughed as we chased that mad animal half way across the county.'

After that, things were easier. I talked about Christmas at Lissadell, and all the fine things I'd seen there, and Hanora told me how she was looking forward to seeing her big brothers and sisters in America.

When we got back to Hanora's house, I didn't want to say goodbye. I didn't know when I'd see her again – lots of people who went to America never came back. Would my dear friend grow up and marry a man I'd never met, and have babies who would grow up to be children with American accents?

'Oh, Hanora,' I said. 'Everything's changing much too fast for me. I don't want you and Rose to leave. I want things to be like they were, with the three of us spending hours together every day.'

She hugged me. 'I know,' she said. 'Sometimes I wish that too, but sometimes ...'

'What?'

'Sometimes I think that change is a good thing.'

'How?'

'Life here isn't fair any more. You've got a good job at Lissadell, but we both know that's not what you want in life. I don't really want to go to America. I'd like to stay here with Mam and Dad – but I can't. There's nothing here for me.'

I didn't understand. 'Why do you say change is a good thing?'

'Don't you see, Lily? Ireland is becoming a different place.'

'How?'

'Before long, women will be allowed to vote. Ireland will be free. There will be opportunities for everyone, not just rich people.'

'Do you really think so? Who told you all this?' I asked, wondering where my quiet friend had got all these new ideas.

'My uncle Maurice has been visiting from Dublin, and the stories he's been telling us ...'

'Like what?'

'He knows a girl who used to be a housemaid in Galway, but she left to work in a drapery store a few years ago. She learned how to make hats, and she saved up all her money, and last month she opened her own little hat shop. Imagine that!'

'Are you telling me the truth?'

'Yes! Trust me, Lily, life won't always be like this. One day you will be free to leave Lissadell and follow your dreams. One day you will be a teacher – just like you always wanted. One day I'll come back from America, and I'll find work here, and have a good life. You and Rose and me, we will all have good lives.'

'One day sounds like a long time away,' I said.

I could hear Hanora's mam calling her for her dinner.

'I have to go,' she said. 'I'll write. I promise I'll write as often as I can.'

'I'll write too,' I said.

'We'll tell each other all the news and it will be almost like having a chat.'

Neither of us believed that for a second, but pretending was easier than facing up to the truth.

We hugged and I went home to Mam and cried in her arms until her shoulder was wet from my tears.

* * *

The walk back to Lissadell seemed to take a long time. I felt as if I was walking away from my old life forever. Despite what she'd said, I couldn't help thinking that I'd never see Hanora again. I'd never play skipping with her or hear her laugh about funny things I said. Would I ever again live with my mam, and see her every day? Would she spend the rest of her life missing me?

But I told myself I shouldn't feel too sad. Denis was growing up and doing a great job of helping Mam. When he moves on, I know Jimmy and Anne and Winnie will in turn step into his shoes. And after that, who knows? Maybe by then, I'll be married with a family of my own, and a little house near Mam, and my own garden and everything. Maybe Hanora was right. Maybe one day I'll be a teacher. Maybe one day won't be too long coming.

The beach was quiet and the sea was grey and peaceful. I stopped walking when I came around the bend and saw Lissadell. Inside the house, I knew Isabelle

and Maggie were waiting to hear the latest funny things Winnie had said. Cook would want to know how Mam liked the cake and the other food she had sent. The Countess had left, and Maeve was sure to be sad, so maybe she'd find me, and pretend-paint me and we could chat. Maybe I could finish Winnie's dress, and get started on one for Anne. Later, Nellie and I would sit in our own little room, and our reading lessons would continue.

I began to walk quickly. It was getting late, and I had a lot to do.

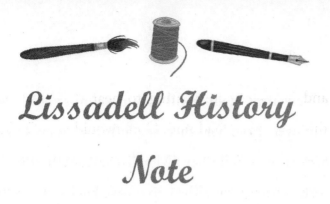

Lissadell History Note

Lily at Lissadell is a mixture of fact and fiction, so I thought I'd write these notes so you can see who really existed, and who came from my (over-active) imagination.

First, I'd like to mention my grandmothers Julianne and Mary Anne – who were very real and very much alive in 1913! Julianne left school at the age of twelve, and went to work as a maid in a house in Cork city. The story about Lily and the Christmas present of winter boots is based on something that happened to Julianne. Mary Anne also left school at a very young age. When she was fourteen she travelled to New York with her sister, looking for work. She found employment as a maid in a large house

in New York State. I still have the dinner service her employers gave her when she left work years later to marry my grandfather. (Married women hardly ever worked back then.) The cup on the back cover of this book is from that tea set, while the one on the front cover is from Julianne's wedding tea set.

I regret that I didn't ask my grandmothers enough questions while they were alive, so if it's not too late, grab your granny (or grandad) and ask them to tell you about their youth.

The House

Lissadell is a real house in County Sligo. It was built in the 1830s for Robert Gore-Booth, and remained in this family until 2003. Over the years, many interesting and famous people have visited, including the poet W.B. Yeats. I visited in the spring of 2019, during my research for this book. It's a beautiful place and if you go there you can see many things mentioned in the book, like the servants' bedrooms, the grand

staircase, the *porte cochere* and the stuffed bear that frightened Lily. You can also see the window where the young Constance Markievicz scratched her name.

The People

Lily and Nellie did not really exist (sorry!) I did a lot of research though, and the lives they lived and the jobs they did are as accurate as I could make them. Many of the other servants were made up too, but quite a few of the people in this book were real. I had a lot of fun researching their stories and putting words in their mouths.

Countess Constance Markievicz

Constance was born in 1868, the eldest of five children. Her sister Eva was her best friend. Constance loved the outdoor life. She enjoyed sailing and was a skilled horsewoman and hunter. She was an accomplished artist – once she did a sketch of a servant in Lissadell. She studied art in London and Paris, where she met her husband Count Markievicz. Initially, she hoped to win votes for women, but then she decided that freedom for Ireland should happen first, saying, 'There can be no free women in an enslaved nation.'

During the 1913 Lockout, she worked hard to establish a soup kitchen to feed poor families. She fought during the 1916 Easter rising and was sentenced to death, but because she was a woman, she was sent to prison instead. She was freed in 1917, and in 1918 she was the first woman ever elected to the British House of Commons. In 1919 she became the Minister for Labour in the Dáil – only the second female minister in the world!

Constance was always generous, and gave most of her wealth to poor people in Dublin. The year before she died she often drove to the country to collect bags of turf, which she gave to families who would otherwise not have been able to heat their homes. When Constance died at the age of fifty-nine, thousands of people came to her funeral.

Maeve de Markievicz

Maeve was Countess Markievicz's only child. She was born in Lissadell House in 1901. Her parents left

her in the care of her grand-mother, Georgina, for most of her childhood, except for a short period when she lived with them in Dublin, along with her half brother Stani-slaus. When she was six she returned to Sligo, and never lived with her parents again. As her Lissadell cousins were much younger, she spent a lot of time with the servants. She liked working in the garden with her Uncle Josslyn, and regularly tried to paint portraits of family members. At the age of sixteen she was sent to boarding school in England, where she became an accomplished violinist. After that she spent little time in Ireland. Some years passed during which she never once saw her mother. When she was twenty, they arranged to meet, but failed to recognise each other, and had to be introduced. (No Instagram or WhatsApp for them!) Maeve trained as a landscape gardener, and also took

up painting again towards the end of her life. Maeve died in England in 1962.

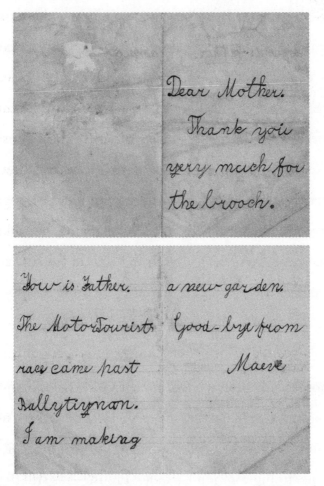

Dear Mother.
Thank you
very much for
the brooch.

How is Father.
The Motor Tourists
race came past
Ballytivnan.
I am making
a new garden.
Good-bye from
Maeve

Maeve wrote this letter to her mother in 1906, when she was five years old.

Sir Josslyn Gore-Booth

Sir Josslyn was Maeve's uncle, and the owner of Lissadell House. His sister, Constance, was older than him, but back then houses and titles went to boys instead of girls! (This wasn't his fault so we shouldn't hold it against him.) He was a good landlord, and worked hard to create employment for local people. He was very interested in horticulture, and developed a number of new daffodil varieties. He was a bit embarrassed by his sister Constance, but when she was sentenced to death, he did all he could to save her.

Butler Kilgallon

Thomas Kilgallon worked for the Gore-Booth family for sixty years, starting when he was ten years old. Count Markievicz did a painting of him on a pillar in the dining room in Lissadell House – it's still there today.

Books about Lily's Time

Since I wasn't alive in 1913(!) I had to read lots of books to find out what Lily's life would have been like. When I first started to think about this book, I knew I'd be writing about a fictional housemaid, but when I discovered *Maeve de Markievicz: Daughter of Constance* by Clive Scoular, my story almost began to write itself. I hadn't known that Countess Markievicz had a daughter, and I was very keen to learn more about her and her life.

These are the other books that I read:

Blazing a Trail by Sarah Webb and Lauren O'Neill

Countess Markievicz: An Adventurous Life by Ann Carroll

Constance Markievicz by Anne Haverty

The Gore-Booths of Lissadell by Dermot James

Revolutionary Lives by Lauren Arrington

I also found lots of useful information on the website www.lissadellhouse.com

Acknowledgements

Thanks to Michael O'Brien who first suggested that I write about the Gore-Booth family and Lissadell House. Big thanks to the current owners of Lissadell House, Edward Walsh and Constance Cassidy, who generously allowed me to visit their home, and shared their huge knowledge of the house and the Gore-Booth family. Thanks to my friend, Sarah Webb, who listened patiently while I worked out early plot details and struggled with a title. Thanks as always to the team at O'Brien Press, who work so hard to bring my books into the world. Special mention has to go to super-editor Helen Carr. Thanks to Rachel Corcoran for another beautiful cover illustration. Thanks to my mum, who shared stories of her mum's early life as a housemaid. Thanks to Dan, and my now scattered children for their ongoing love and support.